Document-Based Questions
Activities

American History

HOLT, RINEHART AND WINSTON

A Harcourt Education Company

Austin • New York • Orlando • Atlanta • San Francisco • Boston • Dallas • Toronto • London

Printed in the United States of America

ISBN 0-03-066534-5

1 2 3 4 5 6 7 8 9   085   04 03 02 01

Contents

Document-Based Questions Activities

Name _____ Class _____ Date _____

Document-Based Essay

Part A

DIRECTIONS Analyze the following documents. Use the documents and your knowledge of American history, to answer the questions that follow each document. Your answers will help you to write a short essay related to the documents.

Document 1

> That this kingdom has the sovereign, the supreme legislative power over America, is granted. It cannot be denied; and taxation is a part of that sovereign power. It is one branch of the legislation. . . .
>   Protection and obedience are reciprocal. Great Britain protects America, America is bound to yield [give] obedience. If not, tell me when the Americans were emancipated? When they want the protection of this kingdom, they are always ready to ask it. That protection has always been afforded them in the most full and ample manner. The nation has run itself into an immense debt to give them this protection; and now they are called upon to contribute a small share to the public expence.
>
>   —George Grenville, Member of Parliament
>   (January 14, 1766)

1a. According to Greenville, why does Great Britain have a large debt? Who should help pay that debt?

_____

_____

_____

1b. Why does Parliament have the power to impose taxes on British colonies, according to Grenville?

_____

_____

_____

Name _____ Class _____ Date _____

Document 2

IMPORTS FROM BRITAIN, 1764–1776

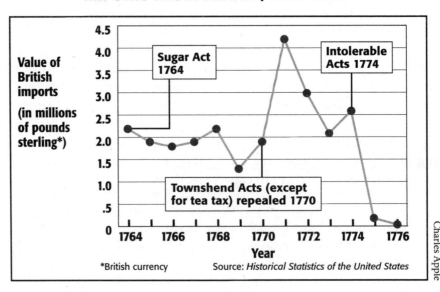

*British currency   Source: *Historical Statistics of the United States*

Charles Apple

2a. Why did imports from Great Britain to the colonies decline?

_____

_____

_____

_____

_____

_____

2b. When did the greatest drop in British imports occur, and why?

_____

_____

_____

_____

_____

_____

Activity 1, The American Revolution, continued

Document 3

> If I was in any doubt, as to the right which the Parliament of Great Britain
> had to tax us without our consent, I should most heartily coincide with you
> in opinion, that to petition, and petition only, is the proper method to apply
> for relief; because we should then be asking a favor, and not claiming a right,
> which, by the law of nature and our constitution, we are, in my opinion,
> indubitably entitled to. I should even think it criminal to go farther than
> this, under such an idea; but none such I have. I think the Parliament of
> Great Britain hath no more right to put their hands into my pockets, with-
> out my consent, than I have to put my hands into yours for money; and this
> being already urged to them in a firm, but decent manner, by all the
> colonies, what reason is there to expect any thing from their justice?
> —George Washington, letter to Bryan Fairfax (July 20, 1774)

3a. Why does Washington believe that just asking the British government to reduce taxes
is the wrong course of action?

_____

_____

_____

_____

_____

_____

_____

3b. According to Washington, what is necessary for Parliament to pass taxes on the
colonists?

_____

_____

_____

_____

_____

_____

_____

Activity 1, The American Revolution, continued

Document 4

> The mother country always considers the colonies . . . as parts of itself; the
> prosperity or unhappiness of either is the prosperity or unhappiness of
> both. . . .
>   Our colonies . . . have been hitherto treated as constituent parts of the
> British Empire. The inhabitants, incorporated by English Charters, are
> entitled to all the rights of Englishmen. They are governed by English laws,
> entitled to English dignities, regulated by English counsels, and protected by
> English arms, and it seems to follow by consequence not easily avoided, that
> they are subject to English government and chargeable by English taxation.
> —Dr. Samuel Johnson (1775)

4a. What is the relationship between England and the colonies, according to Dr. Johnson?

_____

_____

_____

_____

_____

_____

_____

_____

4b. Why does Dr. Johnson believe the colonists ought to pay the taxes imposed on them?

_____

_____

_____

_____

_____

_____

_____

_____

Activity 1, The American Revolution, continued

Document 5

> The resolutions of Parliament breathed a spirit of moderation and forbearance; conciliatory propositions accompanied the measures taken to enforce authority, and the coercive acts were adapted to case of criminal combinations among subjects not then in arms. I have acted with the same temper (spirit), anxious to prevent . . . the effusion [shedding] of the blood of my subjects, and the calamities which are inseparable from a state of war; still hoping that my people in America would have discerned the traitorous views of their leaders, and have been convinced, that to be a subject of Great Britain, with all its consequences, is to be the freest member of any civil society in the known world.
>
> —King George III (October 26, 1775)

5a. Who does the king blame for the disorder in his North American colonies?

_____

_____

_____

_____

_____

_____

5b. What is King George's view of the British government and British society?

_____

_____

_____

_____

_____

_____

_____

Name _____ Class _____ Date _____

Document 6

This recruiting poster was used to recruit soldiers for the Continental Army under the command of General George Washington. For many of those soldiers, this was their first opportunity to meet people from other colonies that were now part of the United States.

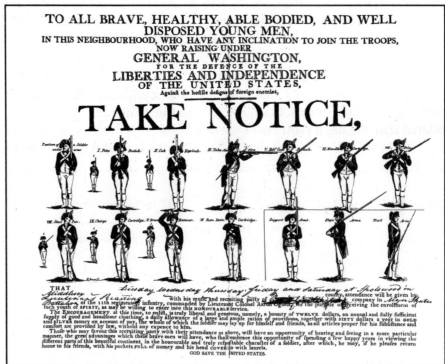

6a. According to the above recruiting poster, why should people sign up to join General Washington's army?

_____

_____

_____

_____

6b. What rewards does the poster promise to those who enlist?

_____

_____

_____

_____

Activity 1, The American Revolution, continued

Document 7

> These are the times that try men's souls. The summer soldier and the sun-
> shine patriot will, in this crisis, shrink from the service of his country, but
> he that stands it *now*, deserves the love and thanks of man and woman.
> Tyranny, like hell, is not easily conquered; yet we have this consolation with
> us, that the harder the conflict, the more glorious the triumph. What we
> obtain too cheap we esteem too lightly; it is dearness only that gives every-
> thing its value. Heaven knows how to put a proper price on its goods; and it
> would be strange indeed if so celestial (heavenly) an article as FREEDOM
> should not be highly rated. Britain, with an army to enforce her tyranny, has
> declared that she has a right (*not only to* TAX) but 'to BIND *us in* ALL
> CASES WHATSOEVER (complete political control); and if being *bound in
> that manner* is not slavery, then there is not such a thing as slavery upon
> earth.
>
> —Thomas Paine, "The Crisis" (1775)

7a. Does Paine provide any evidence to prove England is tyrannical? If so, what?

_____

_____

_____

_____

_____

_____

_____

7b. What does Paine mean by the phrases "sunshine patriot" and "summer soldier"?

_____

_____

_____

_____

_____

_____

_____

Activity 1, The American Revolution, continued

Document 8

> The moderation and virtue of a single character has probably prevented this revolution from being closed as most others have been by a subversion of the liberty it was intended to establish.
> —Thomas Jefferson describing Washington's resignation as commander in chief of the Continental Army

8a. To whom is Jefferson referring to in the above quotation?

_____

_____

_____

_____

_____

_____

_____

_____

_____

_____

8b. Why does Jefferson praise his subject?

_____

_____

_____

_____

_____

_____

_____

_____

_____

_____

_____

_____

Activity 1, The American Revolution, continued

Document-Based Essay

Part B

DIRECTIONS Using the information in the documents provided, and your knowledge of history, write a well-organized essay that includes an introduction, a body of several paragraphs, and a conclusion.

HISTORICAL CONTEXT

Between 1763 and 1775 the relationship between Great Britain and its colonies in North America grew increasingly tense. Ultimately, the colonies would declare their independence and fight a war to become the United States.

TASK

> Using information in the documents and your knowledge of U.S. history, write an essay in which you:
> Describe how the differing points of view held by the British government and many American colonists contributed to their political disagreements. In your essay, include a discussion of how the American colonists responded to actions taken by the British government, the reasons Great Britain pursued its policies despite American opposition, and what brought many Americans to begin to push for independence from Britain.

GUIDELINES

Be sure to:

• Address all aspects of the *Task* by accurately analyzing and interpreting at least <u>four</u> of the documents.

• Use information provided in the documents in the body of your essay.

• Incorporate relevant outside information throughout the essay.

• Support your arguments with facts and information that address the theme.

• Be sure to organize your essay in a clear and logical way.

• Establish a framework that is beyond a simple restatement of the *Task* or *Historical Context*, and conclude the essay with a summation of the theme.

Name _____ Class _____ Date _____

Document-Based Essay

Part A

DIRECTIONS Analyze the following documents. Use the documents and your knowledge of American history to answer the questions that follow each document. Your answers will help you to write a short essay related to the documents.

Document 1

AMERICAN EXPERIMENTS IN SELF GOVERNMENT

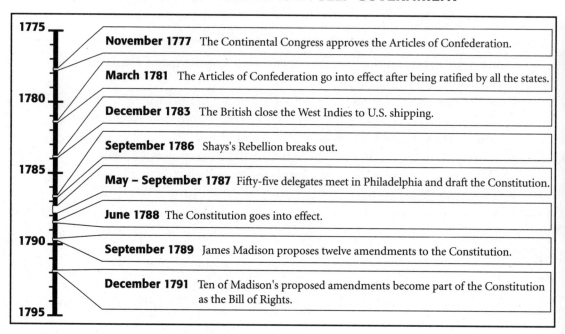

1775

November 1777 The Continental Congress approves the Articles of Confederation.

March 1781 The Articles of Confederation go into effect after being ratified by all the states.

1780

December 1783 The British close the West Indies to U.S. shipping.

September 1786 Shays's Rebellion breaks out.

1785

May – September 1787 Fifty-five delegates meet in Philadelphia and draft the Constitution.

June 1788 The Constitution goes into effect.

1790

September 1789 James Madison proposes twelve amendments to the Constitution.

December 1791 Ten of Madison's proposed amendments become part of the Constitution as the Bill of Rights.

1795

1a. What ongoing event led to the adoption of the Articles of Confederation? When did the Articles of Confederation go into effect?

_____

_____

1b. How many years was the United States governed by the Articles of Confederation?

_____

_____

Activity 2, The Constitutional Convention, continued

Document 2

> We have probably had too good an opinion of human nature in forming our confederation. Experience has taught us, that men will not adopt and carry into execution, measures the best calculated for their own good without the intervention of a coercive power. I do not conceive we can exist long as a nation without having lodged somewhere a power which will pervade the whole Union in as energetic a manner, as the authority of the different state governments extend over the several States. To be fearful of vesting Congress, constituted as that body is, with ample authorities for national purposes, appears to me the very climax of popular absurdity and madness. . . .
>
> What astonishing changes a few years are capable of producing! I am told that even respectable characters speak of a monarchical form of government without horror. From thinking proceeds speaking, thence to acting is often but a single step. But how irrevocable and tremendous! What a triumph for the advocates of despotism to find that we are incapable of governing ourselves, and that systems founded on the basis of equal liberty are merely ideal and fallacious!
>
> —George Washington (August 15, 1786)

2a. What does Washington argue is the problem with the national government under the Articles of Confederation? What must be done to solve the problem in his view?

_____

_____

_____

_____

_____

2b. According to Washington, what has to be taken into account when forming a government?

_____

_____

_____

_____

_____

Activity 2, The Constitutional Convention, continued

Document 3

Resolution of Congress
February 21, 1787

Whereas there is provision in the Articles of Confederation and perpetual Union for making alterations therein by the Assent of a Congress of the United States and of the legislatures of the several States; And whereas experience hath evinced (shown) that there are defects in the present Confederation, as a means to remedy which several of the States and particularly the State of New York by express instruction to their delegates in Congress have suggested a convention for the purposes expressed in the following resolution and such Convention appearing to be the most probable means of establishing in these states a firm national government.

Resolved that in the opinion of Congress it is expedient that on the second Monday in May next a Convention of delegates who shall have been appointed by the several states be held at Philadelphia for the sole and express purpose of revising the Articles of Confederation and provisions therein as shall when agreed to in Congress and confirmed by the states render the federal constitution adequate to the exigencies of Government and the preservation of the Union.

3a. What is the purpose of the convention to be held in Philadelphia in May 1787?

_____

_____

_____

_____

3b. Why is a convention necessary? What demonstrates that such a convention is necessary?

_____

_____

_____

_____

Activity 2, The Constitutional Convention, continued

Document 4

> We the people of the United States, in Order to form a more perfect Union, establish Justice, insure domestic Tranquility, provide for the common defense, promote the general Welfare, and secure the Blessings of Liberty to ourselves and our Posterity, do ordain and establish this Constitution for the United States of America.
>
> —Preamble to the Constitution
> of the United States

4a. According to the Preamble, what is the origin of political power?

_____

_____

_____

_____

_____

_____

_____

_____

_____

4b. Why was the Constitution written, according to the Preamble?

_____

_____

_____

_____

_____

_____

_____

_____

_____

Name _____ Class _____ Date _____

Document 5

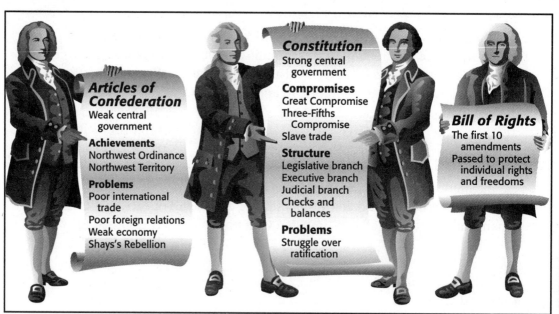

5a. According to the chart, how many branches of government existed under the Articles of Confederation? How many would exist under the Constitution?

_____

_____

_____

_____

_____

_____

5b. What changes introduced in the Constitution indicate that the new government will be more powerful than that under the Articles of Confederation?

_____

_____

_____

_____

_____

_____

_____

Activity 2, The Constitutional Convention, continued

Document 6

> This government (the national government under the Constitution) is to possess absolute and uncontroulable power, legislative, executive and judicial, with respect to every object to which it extends. . . . The powers of the general legislature extend to every case that is of the least importance—there is nothing valuable to human nature, nothing dear to freemen, but what is within its power. It has authority to make laws which will affect the lives, the liberty, and property of every man in the United States; nor can the constitution or laws of any state, in any way prevent or impede (hinder) the full and complete execution of every power given. . . .
>
> (I)t is a truth confirmed by the unerring experience of ages, that every man, and every body of men, invested with power, are ever disposed to increase it, and to acquire a superiority over every thing that stands in their way. This disposition, which is implanted in human nature, will operate in the federal legislature to lessen and ultimately to subvert state authority, and having such advantages, will most certainly succeed, if the federal government succeeds at all.
>
> —"Brutus" (October 18, 1787)

6a. According to Brutus, what is wrong with the government proposed by the Constitution? What branch of government is the most dangerous?

_____

_____

_____

_____

_____

6b. Why must "every body of men" seek to increase their power? What is the source of Brutus' observation?

_____

_____

_____

_____

_____

Name _____ Class _____ Date _____

Activity 2, The Constitutional Convention, continued

Document 7

That the want of a Bill of Rights to accompany this proposed system (the Constitution), is a solid objection to it, provided there is nothing exceptional in the System itself, I do not assert.—If, however, there is at any time, a propriety in having one, it would not have been amiss here. . . . Language is so easy of explanation, and so difficult is it by words to convey exact ideas, that he party to be governed cannot be too explicit. The line cannot be drawn with too much precision and accuracy. The necessity of this accuracy and this precision increases in proportion to the greatness of the sacrifice and the numbers who make it.—That a Constitution for the United States does not require a Bill of Rights, when it is considered, that a Constitution for an individual State would, I cannot conceive.

—"John DeWitt" (October 27, 1787)

7a. What would DeWitt like to see included in the Constitution? Why?

_____

_____

_____

_____

_____

_____

7b. How did supporters of the Constitution respond to arguments such as that put forward by DeWitt?

_____

_____

_____

_____

_____

_____

_____

Document 8

> (T)he great security against a gradual concentration of the several powers
> in the same department (of government), consists in giving to those who
> administer each department, the necessary constitutional means, and per-
> sonal motives, to resist encroachments of the others. The provision for
> defence must in this, as in all cases, be made commensurate (equal) to the
> danger of attack. Ambition must be made to counteract ambition. The
> interest of the man must be connected with the constitutional rights of the
> place. It may be a reflection on human nature, that such devices should be
> necessary should be necessary to controul the abuses of government. But
> what is government itself but the greatest of all reflections of human nature?
> If men were angels, no government would be necessary. . . . In framing a
> government to be administered by men over men, the great difficulty lies in
> this: You must first enable the government to controul the governed; and in
> the next place, oblige it to controul itself. A dependence on the people is no
> doubt the primary controul of government; but experience has taught
> mankind the necessity of auxiliary precautions.
> > —"Publius" (James Madison), *The Federalist No. 51*
> > (February 5, 1788)

8a. What are the two constitutional principles that Madison is referring to in the above
passage from *The Federalist Papers?*

_____

_____

_____

_____

_____

8b. Why is it necessary for the Constitution to create "auxiliary precautions" against the
concentration of power?

_____

_____

_____

_____

_____

(*Activity 2, The Constitutional Convention, continued*)

Document-Based Essay

Part B

DIRECTIONS Using the information in the documents provided and your knowledge of history, write a well-organized essay that includes an introduction, a body of several paragraphs, and a conclusion.

HISTORICAL CONTEXT

Despite gaining independence, the United States had several problems. Unfortunately, the national government under the Articles of Confederation seemed to be too weak to govern. There were commercial disputes between states, Congress lacked the power to levy and collect taxes to pay for national expenses, and Shays's Rebellion was linked to the weaknesses of the national government. As a result, Congress authorized a revision of the Articles of Confederation.

TASK

Using information in the documents and your knowledge of American history, write an essay in which you:

Consider why many people believed a new government was necessary for the United States. Discuss the legitimacy of the document that emerged from the Constitutional Convention in light of the expressed will of Congress and the differences between the Articles of Confederation and the Constitution. Examine the debate over ratification in terms of the objections raised by the Antifederalists and the responses offered by the Federalists. Finally, consider the source of political power and what effect this had on what type of government was created.

GUIDELINES

Be sure to:

• Address all aspects of the *Task* by accurately analyzing and interpreting at least <u>four</u> of the documents.

• Use information provided in the documents in the body of your essay.

• Incorporate relevant outside information in your essay.

• Support your arguments with facts and information that address the theme.

• Be sure to organize your essay in a clear and logical way.

• Establish a framework that is beyond a simple restatement of the *Task* or *Historical Context.*

• Conclude the essay with a summation of the theme.

Name _____ Class _____ Date _____

Document-Based Essay

Part A

DIRECTIONS Analyze the following documents. Use the documents and your knowledge of American history to answer the questions that follow each document. Your answers will help you to write a short essay related to the documents.

Document 1

INDUSTRY IN CONNECTICUT, MASSACHUSETTS, AND RHODE ISLAND, 1850

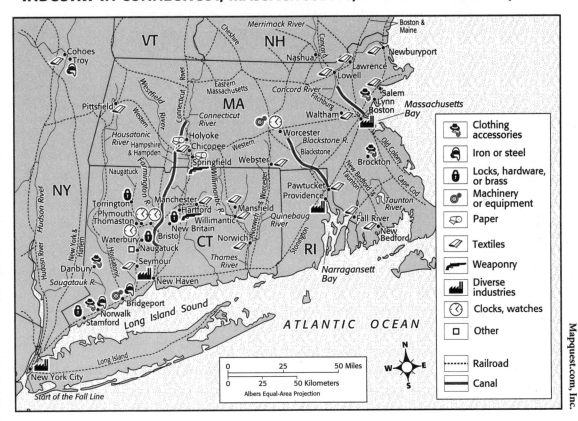

1a. What geographic feature indicated on the map is common to the industrial centers?

_____

1b. What effect did the development of railroads have upon industry in the United States?

_____

Name _____ Class _____ Date _____

Document 2

GROWTH IN URBAN POPULATION, 1800–1860

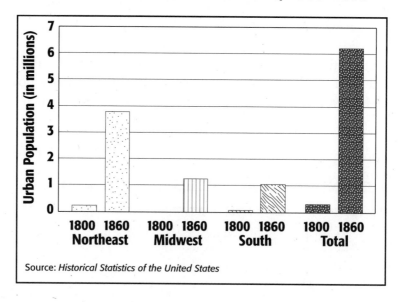

Source: *Historical Statistics of the United States*

2a. Which region of the country experienced the greatest increase in urban growth between 1800 and 1860?

_____

_____

_____

_____

_____

_____

2b. Why was urban growth uneven across different regions of the country? What political effect did this have on the United States?

_____

_____

_____

_____

_____

_____

_____

Activity 3, The First Industrial Revolution, continued

Document 3

> It is only half a century since the United States has escaped from the colonial dependence in which England held it; there are few great fortunes there and capital is still scarce. But no other nation has made as rapid progress in trade and industry as the Americans.
>
> In the United States the greatest industrial undertakings are executed without trouble because the whole population is engaged in industry and because the poorest man as well as the most opulent gladly joins forces therein. . . .
>
> The Americans make great advances in industry because they are all at the same time engaged in it, and for this same reason they are subject to very unexpected and formidable industrial crises.
>
> As they are all engaged in trade, trade is affected by such various and complex causes that it is impossible to foresee what embarrassments may arise. As they are all more or less engaged in industry, at the least shock given to business activity all private fortunes are in jeopardy at the same time and the state is shaken.
>
> —Alexis de Tocqueville, *Democracy in America*

From *Democracy in America* by Alexis de Tocqueville, edited by J.P. Mayer, translated by George Lawrence. Translation copyright©1966 by **Harper Collins Publishers, Inc.** Reprinted by permission of the publisher.

3a. According to Tocqueville, who in the United States is engaged in industry?

_____

_____

_____

_____

_____

3b. What danger does Tocqueville see in American industry?

_____

_____

_____

_____

_____

_____

Activity 3, The First Industrial Revolution, continued

Document 4

> At the time the Lowell cotton mills were started the caste of the factory girl was the lowest among the employments of women. In England and in France, particularly, great injustice had been done to her real character. She was represented as subjected to influences that must destroy her purity and self-respect. In the eyes of her overseer she was but a brute, a slave, to be beaten, pinched and pushed about. It was to overcome this prejudice that such high wages had been offered to women that they might be induced to become mill girls, in spite of the opprobrium (bad reputation) that still clung to this degrading occupation. . . . The most prevailing incentive to labor was to secure the means of education for some *male* member of the family. To make a *gentleman* of a brother or a son, to give him a college education, was the dominant thought in the minds of a great many of the better class of mill girls. I have known more than one to give every cent of her wages, month after month, to her brother, that he might get the education necessary to enter some profession. I have known a mother to work years in this way for her boy. I have known women to educate young men by their earnings, who were not sons or relatives. There are many men now living who were helped to an education by the wages of the early mill-girls.
> —Harriet Robinson, "Early Factory Labor in New England" (1883)

4a. According to Robinson, why did many mill girls take jobs in the Lowell textile mills?

_____

_____

_____

_____

_____

4b. What did the Lowell mills offer to help overcome the popular image of working women in the early 1800s?

_____

_____

_____

_____

_____

Name _____ Class _____ Date _____

Document 5

> A very good Hand Weaver, a man twenty-five or thirty years of age, will weave two pieces of nine-eighths shirting per week, each twenty four yards long, and containing one hundred and five shoots of weft in an inch, the reed of the cloth being a forty-four, Bolton count, and the warp and weft forty hanks to the pound. A Steam Loom Weaver, fifteen years of age, will in the same time weave seven similar pieces. A Steam Loom factory containing two hundred Looms, with the assistance of one hundred persons under twenty years of age, and of twenty-five men will weave seven hundred pieces per week. . . . To manufacture one hundred similar pieces per week by the hand, it would be necessary to employ at least one hundred and twenty-five Looms. . . . It requires a man of mature age and a very good Weaver to weave two of the pieces in a week, and there is also an allowance to be made for sickness and other incidents. Thus, eight hundred and seventy-five hand Looms would be required to produce the seven hundred pieces per week; and reckoning the weavers, with their children, and the aged and infirm belonging to them at two and a half to each loom, it may very safely be said, that the work done in a Steam Factory containing two hundred Looms, would, if done by hand Weavers, find employment and support for a population of more than two thousand persons.
>
> —Richard Guest (1823)

5a. Which method of weaving described by Guest is more efficient at producing cloth?

_____

_____

_____

_____

_____

5b. What is the negative effect of industrialization on textile workers according to the passage?

_____

_____

_____

_____

_____

Name _____ Class _____ Date _____

Document 6

TIME TABLE OF THE LOWELL MILLS,

Arranged to make the working time throughout the year average 11 hours per day.

TO TAKE EFFECT SEPTEMBER 21st., 1853.

The Standard time being that of the meridian of Lowell, as shown by the Regulator Clock of AMOS SANBORN, Post Office Corner, Central Street.

From March 20th to September 19th, inclusive.

COMMENCE WORK, at 6.30 A. M. LEAVE OFF WORK, at 6.30 P. M., except on Saturday Evenings.
BREAKFAST at 6 A. M. DINNER, at 12 M. Commence Work, after dinner, 12.45 P. M.

From September 20th to March 19th, inclusive.

COMMENCE WORK at 7.00 A. M. LEAVE OFF WORK, at 7.00 P. M., except on Saturday Evenings.
BREAKFAST at 6.30 A. M. DINNER, at 12.30 P.M. Commence Work, after dinner, 1.15 P. M.

BELLS.

From March 20th to September 19th, inclusive.

Morning Bells.	Dinner Bells.	Evening Bells.
First bell,............4.30 A. M.	Ring out,..............12.00 M.	Ring out,............6.30 P. M.
Second, 5.30 A. M.; Third, 6.20.	Ring in,...............12.35 P. M.	Except on Saturday Evenings.

From September 20th to March 19th, inclusive.

Morning Bells.	Dinner Bells.	Evening Bells.
First bell,............5.00 A. M.	Ring out,..............12.30 P. M.	Ring out at............7.00 P. M.
Second, 6.00 A. M.; Third, 6.50.	Ring in,...............1.05 P. M.	Except on Saturday Evenings.

SATURDAY EVENING BELLS.

During APRIL, MAY, JUNE, JULY, and AUGUST. Ring Out, at 6.00 P. M.
The remaining Saturday Evenings in the year, ring out as follows :

SEPTEMBER.	NOVEMBER.	JANUARY.
First Saturday, ring out 6.00 P. M.	Third Saturday ring out 4.00 P. M.	Third Saturday, ring out 4.25 P. M.
Second " " 5.45 "	Fourth " " 3.55 "	Fourth " " 4.35 "
Third " " 5.30 "	DECEMBER.	FEBRUARY.
Fourth " " 5.20 "	First Saturday, ring out 3.50 P. M.	First Saturday, ring out 4.45 P. M.
OCTOBER.	Second " " 3.55 "	Second " " 4.55 "
First Saturday, ring out 5.05 P. M.	Third " " 3.55 "	Third " " 5.00 "
Second " " 4.55 "	Fourth " " 4.00 "	Fourth " " 5.10 "
Third " " 4.45 "	Fifth " " 4.00 "	MARCH.
Fourth " " 4.35 "		First Saturday, ring out 5.25 P. M.
Fifth " " 4.25 "		Second " " 5.30 "
NOVEMBER.	JANUARY.	Third " " 5.35 "
First Saturday, ring out 4.15 P. M.	First Saturday, ring out 4.10 P. M.	Fourth " " 5.45 "
Second " " 4.05 "	Second " " 4.15 "	

YARD GATES will be opened at the first stroke of the bells for entering or leaving the Mills.

*** SPEED GATES commence hoisting three minutes before commencing work.

American Textile History Museum

6a. What time are the workers expected to be at work, and what time are they allowed to leave?

_____

_____

_____

_____

_____

6b. Why would the Lowell mill have a different schedule from March 20 to September 19 than the schedule from September 20 to March 19?

_____

_____

_____

_____

Activity 3, The First Industrial Revolution, continued

Document 7

THE MCCORMICK REAPER

Archive Photos

The *London Times* described the McCormick reaper, which was designed to harvest wheat, as "a cross between a flying machine [and] a wheelbarrow."

7a. How would the use of the McCormick reaper make a farmer's life easier and more profitable?

_____

_____

_____

_____

_____

7b. What was the effect of the Industrial Revolution on agriculture in the United States? How is that illustrated by the McCormick reaper?

_____

_____

_____

_____

_____

Activity 3, The First Industrial Revolution, continued

Document 8

> The expediency of encouraging manufactures in the United States, which was not long since deemed very questionable, appears at this time to be pretty generally admitted. The embarrassments which have obstructed the progress of our external trade, have led to serious reflections on the necessity of enlarging the sphere (increasing the amount) of our domestic commerce. The restrictive regulations, which, in foreign markets, abridge (stop) the vent (selling) of the increasing surplus of our agricultural produce, serve to beget (create) an earnest (sincere) desire that a more extensive demand for the surplus may be created at home; and the complete success which has rewarded manufacturing enterprise in some valuable branches, conspiring (together) with the promising symptoms which attend some less mature essays (attempts) in others, justify a hope that the obstacles to the growth of this species (type) of industry are less formidable than they were apprehended thought to be. . . .
>
> —Alexander Hamilton, "Report on Manufactures" (1791)

8a. What reason does Hamilton give for the U.S. government to encourage the development of manufacturing?

_____

_____

_____

_____

_____

_____

8b. What effect will the development of industry have on the economy of the United States, according to Hamilton?

_____

_____

_____

_____

_____

_____

Activity 3, The First Industrial Revolution, continued

Document-Based Essay

Part B

DIRECTIONS Using the information in the documents provided and your knowledge of history, write a well-organized essay that includes an introduction, a body of several paragraphs, and a conclusion.

HISTORICAL CONTEXT
Thomas Jefferson saw the future of the United States in the development of agriculture, however, his prediction did not come true. Beginning in the early 1800s, the United States experienced an industrial revolution that transformed the American economy and society.

TASK

> Using information in the documents and your knowledge of American history, write an essay in which you:
> Explain why Alexander Hamilton argued in favor of the development of manufacturing in the United States and assess whether or not he was correct in his assertions regarding the effect that the encouragement of the industry would have on the country. Consider the geographic factors that led industry to develop where it did and how this affected population distribution. Finally, discuss what effect the Industrial Revolution had on workers and farmers in the United States.

GUIDELINES:

Be sure to:

- Address all aspects of the *Task* by accurately analyzing and interpreting at least <u>four</u> of the documents.

- Use information provided in the documents in the body of your essay.

- Incorporate relevant outside information in your essay.

- Support your arguments with facts and information that address the theme.

- Be sure to organize your essay in a clear and logical way.

- Establish a framework that is beyond a simple restatement of the *Task* or *Historical Context.*

- Conclude the essay with a summation of the theme.

ACTIVITY **4**

Document-Based Questions

Slavery and the Civil War

Document-Based Essay

Part A

DIRECTIONS Analyze the following documents. Use the documents and your knowledge of American history to answer the questions that follow each document. Your answers will help you to write a short essay related to the documents.

Document 1

> **Col. Mason.** Slavery discourages arts and manufactures. The poor despise labor when performed by slaves. . . . Every master of slaves is born a petty tyrant. They bring the judgment of heaven on a Country. As nations cannot be rewarded or punished in the next world they must be in this. By an inevitable chain of causes and effects providence punishes national sins by national calamities.
>
> **Mr. Elsworth.** Let us not intermeddle. As population increases poor laborers will be so plenty as to render slaves useless. Slavery in time will not be a speck in our Country.
>
> —Debate in the Constitutional Convention (August 27, 1787)

1a. What does Elsworth believe the Constitution ought to say about slavery? Why?

_____

_____

_____

_____

_____

1b. Why does Mason believe that failure to address the question of slavery is dangerous?

_____

_____

_____

_____

_____

Activity 4, Slavery and the Civil War, continued

Document 2

> One man will clean ten times as much cotton as he can in any other way
> before known and also clean it much better than in the usual mode. This
> machine may be turned with water or with a horse, with the greatest ease,
> and man and a horse will do more than fifty men with the old machines.
> —Eli Whitney, commenting on the cotton gin (1793)

2a. What does Whitney claim his new machine will make possible?

_____

_____

_____

_____

_____

_____

_____

_____

2b. What effect did the cotton gin have on agriculture in the South? What did this mean
for the institution of slavery?

_____

_____

_____

_____

_____

_____

_____

_____

_____

Activity 4, Slavery and the Civil War, continued

Document 3

THE MISSOURI COMPROMISE, 1820

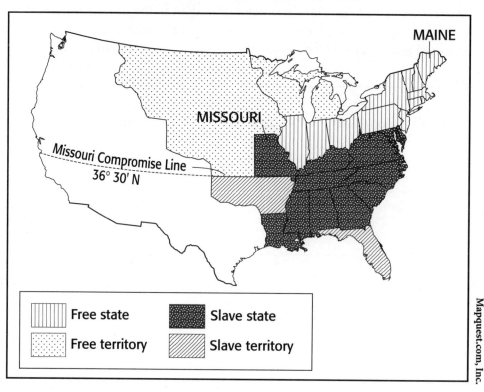

Mapquest.com, Inc.

3a. After the Missouri Compromise, how many slave states were there? How many free states?

_____

_____

_____

_____

_____

_____

3b. What was the purpose of the Missouri Compromise?

_____

_____

_____

_____

Activity 4, Slavery and the Civil War, continued

Document 4

> We, (coloured people of these United States of America) are the *most wretched, degraded* and *abject* [lowly] set of beings that *ever lived* since the world began, and that the white Americans having reduced us to this wretched state of *slavery*, treat us in that condition *more cruel* (they being an enlightened and Christian people) than any heathen nation did any people whom it had reduced to our condition. These affirmations are so well confirmed in the minds of unprejudiced men, who have taken the trouble to read histories, that they need no elucidation from me. . . .
>
> —David Walker, "An Appeal to the Colored Citizens of the World" (1829)

4a. According to Walker, what is the condition of African Americans in the United States?

_____

_____

_____

_____

_____

_____

_____

_____

4b. How did African Americans reach this condition?

_____

_____

_____

_____

_____

_____

_____

_____

_____

Activity 4, Slavery and the Civil War, continued

Document 5

> Domestic slavery in the Southern States has produced the same results in elevating the character of the master that it did in Greece and Rome. He is lofty and independent in his sentiments, generous, affectionate, brave and eloquent; he is superior to the Northerner in every thing but the arts of thrift. . . . But the chief and most important enquiry is, how does slavery affect the condition of the slave? We provide for each slave, in old age and in infancy, in sickness and in health, not according to his labor, but according to his wants. . . . There is no rivalry, no competition to get employment among slaves, as among free laborers. Nor is there war between master and slave.
>
> —George Fitzhugh, *Sociology for the South* (1854)

5a. According to Fitzhugh, who benefits from the existence of slavery in the South? What does this indicate about Fitzhugh's perspective on the question of slavery?

_____

_____

_____

_____

_____

_____

_____

5b. Using Fitzhugh's argument, who has better conditions, the free laborer in the North or the slave in the South? Why?

_____

_____

_____

_____

_____

_____

_____

Activity 4, *Slavery and the Civil War,* continued

Document 6

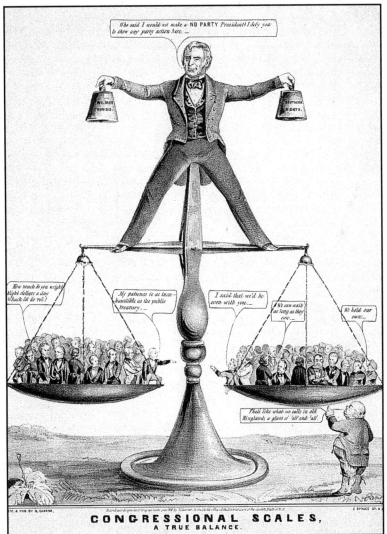

CONGRESSIONAL SCALES,
A TRUE BALANCE.

6a. What do the scales represent?

_____

_____

_____

6b. What is President Taylor trying to do?

_____

_____

_____

Name _____ Class _____ Date _____

Document 7

SOUTHERN AGRICULTURE AND THE SLAVE TRADE, 1860

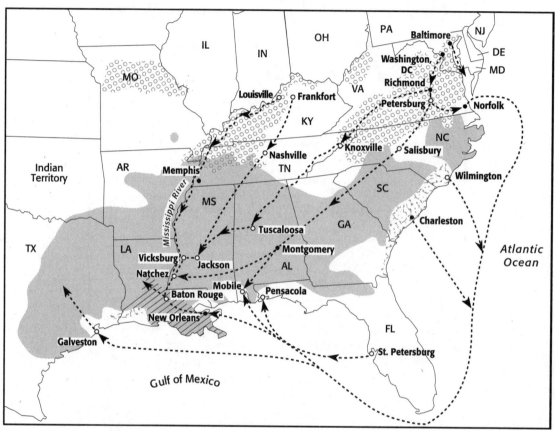

7a. According to the map, what was the primary crop in the South?

_____

_____

_____

_____

7b. How does the map indicate the westward expansion of southern agriculture?

_____

_____

_____

_____

Activity 4, Slavery and the Civil War, continued

Document 8

> If we could first know where we are, and whither we are tending (where we
> are going), we could better judge what to do, and how to do it. We are now
> far into fifth year since a policy was initiated with the avowed object and
> confident promise of putting an end to slavery agitation (the *Dred Scott*
> decision). Under the operation of that policy, that agitation has not only not
> ceased, but has been constantly augmented (added to). In my opinion, it will
> not cease until a crisis shall have been reached and passed. "A house divided
> against itself cannot stand." I believe this government cannot endure perma-
> nently half slave and half free. I do not expect the Union to be dissolved;
> I do not expect the house to fall; but I do expect it will cease to be divided.
> It will become all one thing, or all the other. Either the opponents of slavery
> will arrest the further spread of it, and place it where the public mind shall
> rest in the belief that it is in the course of ultimate extinction, or its advo-
> cates will push it forward till it shall become alike lawful in all the States,
> old as well as new, North as well as South.
>
> —Abraham Lincoln, (1858)

8a. To what is Lincoln referring to when he describes a "house divided"?

_____

_____

_____

_____

_____

_____

8b. How accurate was Lincoln's prediction that the "house" would cease to be divided?

_____

_____

_____

_____

_____

_____

Activity 4, Slavery and the Civil War, continued

Document-Based Essay

Part B

DIRECTIONS Using the information in the documents provided and your knowledge of history, write a well-organized essay that includes an introduction, a body of several paragraphs, and a conclusion.

HISTORICAL CONTEXT

From the inception of the United States, the question of slavery posed a particular problem. The Declaration of Independence had declared that "all men are created equal," yet at the same time the United States had a large population of human beings held as slaves. The fact that by the early 1800s slavery was largely confined to the South made this problem a source of conflict between regions of the country. It also led to differing perspectives on the question of slavery itself.

TASK

> Using information in the documents and your knowledge of American history, write an essay in which you:
> Explain what attitude many of the founders of the United States took with regard to the institution of slavery and its effects on both the slave and the slaveholder and the ways in which those original conceptions were transformed by historical developments in the United States. In your essay, include discussion of important events, political efforts, and arguments advanced regarding the issue of slavery.

GUIDELINES:

Be sure to:

• Address all aspects of the *Task* by accurately analyzing and interpreting at least <u>four</u> of the documents.

• Use information provided in the documents in the body of your essay.

• Incorporate relevant outside information in your essay.

• Support your arguments with facts and information that address the theme.

• Be sure to organize your essay in a clear and logical way.

• Establish a framework that is beyond a simple restatement of the *Task* or *Historical Context*.

• Conclude the essay with a summation of the theme.

Name _____ Class _____ Date _____

Document-Based Questions
The West

Document-Based Essay

Part A

DIRECTIONS Analyze the following documents. Use the documents and your knowledge of American history to answer the questions that follow each document. Your answers will help you to write a short essay related to the documents.

Document 1

> Texas has been absorbed into the Union in the inevitable fulfillment of the general law which is rolling our population westward. . . . It was disintegrated form Mexico in the natural course of events, by a process perfectly legitimate on its own part, blameless on ours. . . . (its) incorporation into the Union was not only inevitable, but the most natural, right and proper thing in the world. . . . California will, probably, next fall away from . . . Mexico. . . . A population will soon be in actual occupation of California, over which it will be idle for Mexico to dream of dominion. . . . All this without agency of our government, without responsibility of our people in the natural flow of events, the spontaneous working of principles, and the adaptation of the tendencies and wants of the human race to the elemental circumstances in the midst of which they find themselves placed.
>
> The American claim is by the right of our manifest destiny to overspread and to possess the whole of the continent which Providence [fate] has given us for the development of the great experiment of liberty.
> —John L. O'Sullivan, editor of the *Democratic Review* (1845)

1a. According to O'Sullivan, what is "manifest destiny"?

_____

_____

_____

1b. What is the purpose of manifest destiny according to O'Sullivan?

_____

_____

_____

Activity 5, The West, continued

Document 2

2a. According to the poster above, what is being given away?

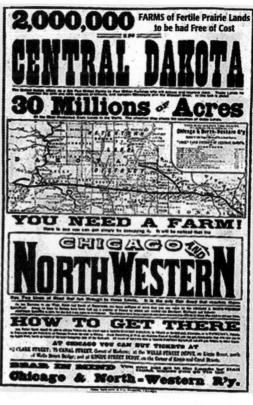

_____

_____

_____

_____

_____

_____

_____

_____

_____

_____

_____

2b. Why would it be given away for free? What does the railroad company have to gain by advertising it?

_____

_____

_____

_____

_____

_____

_____

_____

_____

_____

Activity 5, The West, continued

Document 3

(In her novel, O Pioneers! *[1913], Willa Cather gave an accurate portrayal of what life was like for those people who moved West and settled the Great Plains.)*

On one of the ridges of that wintry waste stood the low log house in which John Bergson was dying. . . .

In eleven long years John Bergson had made but little impression upon the wild land he had come to tame. It was still a wild thing that had its ugly moods; and no one knew when they were likely to come, or why. Mischance hung over it. Its Genius was unfriendly to man. . . .

Bergson went over in his mind the things that had held him back. One winter his cattle had perished in a blizzard. The next summer one of his plow horses broke its leg in a prairie-dog hole and had to be shot. Another summer he lost his hogs from cholera, and a valuable stallion died from a rattlesnake bite. Time and again his crops had failed. He had lost two children, boys, that came between Lou and Emil, and there had been the cost of sickness and death. Now, when he had at last struggled out of debt, he was going to die himself. He was only forty-six, and had, of course, counted upon more time.

Bergson had spent his first five years on the Divide getting into debt, and the last six getting out. He had paid off his mortgages and had ended pretty much where he began, with the land.

3a. What was life on the Plains like for Bergson?

_____

_____

_____

_____

3b. What misfortunes befell Bergson, and what did he gain from the experience?

_____

_____

_____

_____

Activity 5, The West, continued

Document 4

> In the total absence of any argument that can justify the war in which we are now involved, resort has been [made] to a most extraordinary assertion [claim]. It is said that the people of the United States have a hereditary superiority of race over the Mexicans, which gives them the right to subjugate [oppress] and keep in bondage the inferior nation. This, it is also alleged [claimed], will be the means of enlightening the degraded Mexicans, of improving their social state, and of ultimately increasing the happiness of the masses. . . .
>
> Among ourselves the most ignorant, the most inferior, either in physical or mental faculties, is recognized as having equal, and he has an equal vote with anyone, however superior to him in all those respects. This is founded on the immutable [unchangeable] principle that no man is born with the right of governing another man. . . .
>
> The same principle will apply to nations. . . . The people of the United States may rightfully, and will, if they use the proper means exercise a most beneficial moral influence over the Mexicans and other less enlightened nations of America. Beyond this they have no right to go.
>
> —Albert Gallatin, *Peace with Mexico* (1847)

4a. What idea is Gallatin arguing against?

_____

_____

_____

_____

_____

4b. Instead of conquering Mexico and taking territory, what is Gallatin arguing in favor of?

_____

_____

_____

_____

_____

Activity 5, The West, *continued*

Document 5

> (A) railroad, from some point on the Mississippi, or its tributaries, to some
> point on the bay of San Francisco, is the best route that can be adopted for
> the purpose of securing the Commerce of China and India; . . . to open a
> great national highway from California to the Atlantic coast, [and] would be
> a greater defence and protection than all other military works. It would also
> be the means of great daily intercourse between the East and West coast of
> this Republic, . . . to prevent those sectional feelings which have ever been
> the destruction of wide-extended governments. . . . [I]t is the duty of this
> Legislature to encourage the speedy building of a Railroad from the Atlantic
> to the Pacific, across the territory of the United States.
> —J.J. Warner, Report on Railroads to the California Senate (1851)

5a. What are the reasons Warner gives for constructing a transcontinental railroad?

_____

_____

_____

_____

_____

_____

_____

5b. Who is responsible for encouraging the building of such a railroad, according to
Warner?

_____

_____

_____

_____

_____

_____

_____

(Activity 5, The West, continued)

Document 6

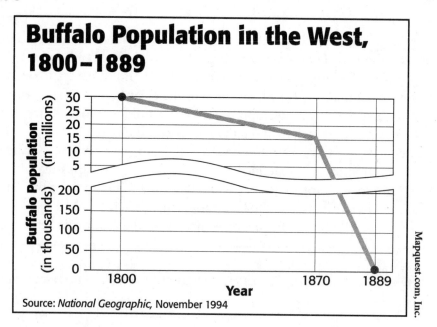

6a. By how much did the buffalo population in the West decline between 1870 and 1889?

_____

_____

_____

_____

_____

_____

6b. What was the cause of the decline in the buffalo population? What effect did this have on the Plains Indians?

_____

_____

_____

_____

_____

_____

_____

_____

Name _____ Class _____ Date _____

Activity 5, The West, continued

Document 7

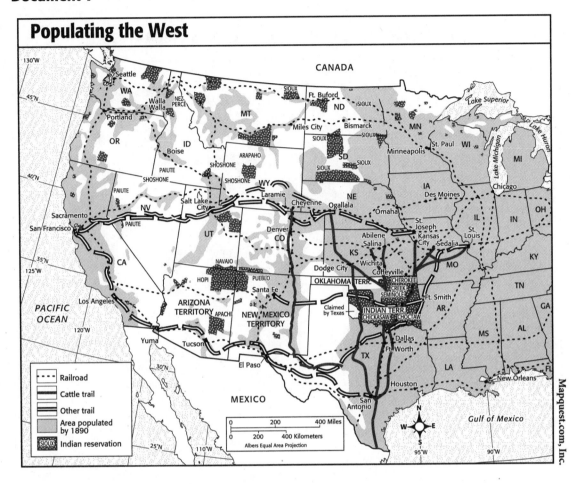

Populating the West

Legend:
- - - - Railroad
═══ Cattle trail
──── Other trail
▓▓ Area populated by 1890
▨ Indian reservation

7a. What man-made features correspond with settlements in the West?

_____

_____

_____

_____

7b. Why would California be more heavily populated than other Western states and territories?

_____

_____

_____

_____

Activity 5, The West, continued

Document 8

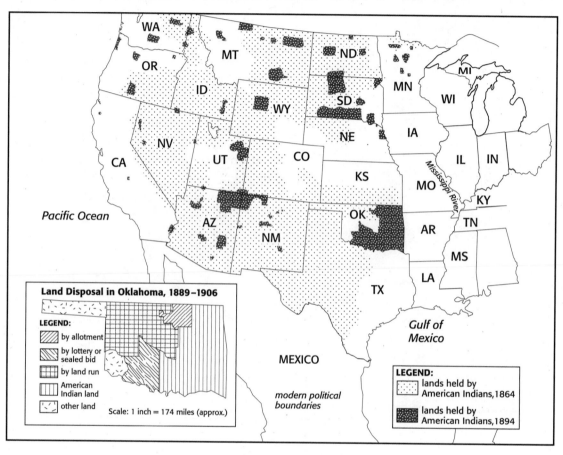

SHRINKING AMERICAN INDIAN LANDS, 1864–1894

8a. In what two states did American Indians lose all their land between 1864 and 1894? Which state continued to have a large area of American Indian land in 1894?

_____

_____

_____

8b. In which states west of the Mississippi River did American Indians have no lands in 1864? Why not?

_____

_____

_____

Document-Based Essay

Part B

DIRECTIONS Using the information in the documents provided and your knowledge of history, write a well-organized essay that includes an introduction, a body of several paragraphs, and a conclusion.

HISTORICAL CONTEXT
Beginning the mid-1800s more and more Americans began to move into the frontier of the West. There were many reasons for people to settle in the West, the availability of land for farming, gold and other minerals for the creation of mines, businesses to serve the needs of a growing population, and so on. Many people believed that it was the destiny of the United States to stretch from the Atlantic Ocean to the Pacific Ocean.

TASK

> Using information in the documents and your knowledge of American history, write an essay in which you:
> Explain the reasons for the rapid settlement of the West that began in the middle of the 1800s, including a discussion of the idea of manifest destiny and the Mexican War. Consider what effect the settlement of the West had upon the ways of life of the American Indians who lived there and the American settlers. Finally, discuss the importance of the transcontinental railroad to the development of the western frontier.

GUIDELINES
Be sure to:

- Address all aspects of the *Task* by accurately analyzing and interpreting at least <u>four</u> of the documents.

- Use information provided in the documents in the body of your essay.

- Incorporate relevant outside information in your essay.

- Support your arguments with facts and information that address the theme.

- Be sure to organize your essay in a clear and logical way.

- Establish a framework that is beyond a simple restatement of the *Task* or *Historical Context*. Conclude the essay with a summation of the theme.

(ACTIVITY 6) Document-Based Questions

Immigration and Urbanization

Document-Based Essay

Part A

DIRECTIONS Analyze the following documents. Use the documents and your knowledge of American history to answer the questions that follow each document. Your answers will help you to write a short essay related to the documents.

Document

SHIFTING PATTERNS OF IMMIGRATION

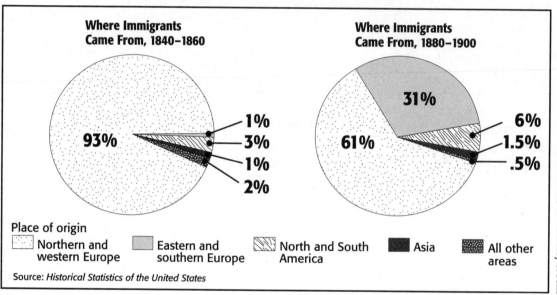

Where Immigrants Came From, 1840–1860

93%
1%
3%
1%
2%

Where Immigrants Came From, 1880–1900

31%
61%
6%
1.5%
.5%

Place of origin

Northern and western Europe   Eastern and southern Europe   North and South America   Asia   All other areas

Source: *Historical Statistics of the United States*

Dave Merrell/Steven Edsey & Sons

1a. What group accounted for the greatest increase in immigration between 1840–60 and 1880–90?

_____

_____

1b. What was the reaction of many Americans to the changing patterns of immigration to the United States?

_____

_____

Activity 6, Immigration and Urbanization, continued

Document 2

> We began to make inquiries about jobs and were promptly informed that there was plenty of work at "pick and shovel." We were also given to understand by our fellow-boarders that "pick and shovel" was practically the only work available to Italians. . . . I practiced for a day until I could say "peek" and "shuvle" to perfection. . . .
>
> One morning . . . we saw a fat man coming toward us. "Buon giorno [good morning], padrone," said one of the men. "Padrone?" I said to myself. Now the word "padrone" in Italy is applied to a proprietor, geerally a respectable man. . . . This man not only showed no signs of good breeding in his face, but he as unshaven and dirty and his clothes were shabby. . . .
>
> The "padrone" came up to our group and began to wax (talk) eloquent and to gesticulate (gesture) . . . about the advantages of a certain job. . . . "It is not very far, only twelve miles from Boston. . . . The company has a 'shantee' in which you can sleep and a 'storo' where you can buy your 'grosserie' all very cheap. Buono paga (good pay) . . . $1.25 a day, and you only have to pay me fifty cents a week for having gotten you this 'gooda jobbaz.'. . .
>
> On reaching our destination we were taken to the "shantee" where we were introduced to two long open bunkss filled with straw. The "storo" . . . was at one end of the shanty. . . . We began to do some simple figuring and discovered that when had paid for our groceries . . . for the privilege of sleeping in the shanty, and the fifty cents to the "padrone" for having been so condescending as to employ us, we would have nothing left but sore arms and backs.
>
> —Constantine Panunzio came to the United States in 1902.

2a. What kinds of jobs were available to many immigrants to the United States at the end of the 1800s and the beginning of the 1900s according to the passage?

_____

_____

_____

2b. Was the "padrone" fair to Panunzio and his friend? Explain your answer.

_____

_____

_____

Activity 6, Immigration and Urbanization, continued

Document 3

> I dreamed of golden stairs leading to the top of the American palace where father was supposed to live. (I) went "home" to . . . an ugly old tenement in the heart of the Lower East Side. There were stairs to climb but they were not golden.
>
> —Anonymous immigrant girl

3a. What was the difference between the immigrant girl's dream of America and the reality she encountered?

_____

_____

_____

_____

_____

_____

_____

_____

_____

3b. What type of help was available to immigrants to deal with the realities of American life? Who provided the assistance?

_____

_____

_____

_____

_____

_____

_____

_____

_____

_____

Activity 6, Immigration and Urbanization, continued

Document 4

Look at the "dens of death" in Baxter Street . . . says the health inspector, "into which the sunlight never enters . . . that are dark, damp, dismal throughout all the days of the year, and for which it is no exaggeration to say that the money paid to the owners as rent is literally the 'price of blood.'". . . The mortality officially registered in those "dens of death" was 17.5 percent of their population. . . . Bedrooms in tenements were dark closets, utterly without ventilation. There couldn't be any. The houses were built like huge square boxes, covering nearly the whole of the lot. Some light came in at the ends, but the middle was always black. Forty thousand windows, cut by order of the Health Board that first year, gave us a daylight view of the slum: "damp and rotten and dark," walls and banisters sticky with constant moisture.
—Jacob Riis, *How the Other Half Lives* (1890)

4a. Why does Riis describe the tenements in which many immigrants live as "dens of death"?

_____

_____

_____

_____

_____

_____

_____

4b. What were living conditions like in many tenements as described by Riis?

_____

_____

_____

_____

_____

_____

_____

Name _____ Class _____ Date _____

Document 5

The Granger Collection, New York

5a. What is happening in the political cartoon above?

_____

_____

_____

_____

_____

_____

5b. Do you think that the cartoonist supported increased immigration? Explain your answer.

_____

_____

_____

_____

_____

_____

_____

Name _____ Class _____ Date _____

Document 6

> When I was sixteen, I was supposed to marry a man in Italy, but I didn't want him. My mama tell me, "Either you marry this guy or you go to America." But I told her, "I don't like him." She say, "Then you go to America." That's why I came to America. There was nothing in Italy, nothing in Italy. That's why we came. To find work, because Italy didn't have no work. Mama used to say, "America is rich, America is rich."
>
> —Carla Martinelli

6a. Why did Martinelli leave Italy to go to the United States?

_____

_____

_____

_____

_____

_____

_____

_____

6b. Why did Martinelli's mother tell her to move to the United States?

_____

_____

_____

_____

_____

_____

_____

_____

_____

Name _____ Class _____ Date _____

Document 7

THROWING DOWN THE LADDER BY WHICH THEY ROSE.

Courtesy of Strong Museum, Rochester, New York

7a. How does the cartoon above make fun of the nativist response to Chinese immigration?

_____

_____

_____

_____

_____

_____

7b. Why did many nativists oppose Chinese immigration?

_____

_____

_____

_____

_____

_____

_____

52 Document-Based Activities

Activity 6, Immigration and Urbanization, continued

Document 8

The Settlement then, is an experimental effort to aid in the solution of the social and industrial problems which are engendered [created] by the modern conditions of life in a great city. It insists that these problems are not confined to any one portion of a city. It is an attempt to relieve, at the same time, the overaccumulation at one end of society and the destitution [poverty] at the other; but it assumes that this overaccumulation and destitution is most sorely felt in the things that pertain to social and educational privileges. From its very nature it can stand for no political or social propaganda. It must, in a sense, give the warm welcome of an inn to all such propaganda, if perchance one of them be found an angel. The only thing to be dreaded in the Settlement is that it lose its flexibility, its power of quick adaptation, its readiness to change its methods as its environment may demand. It must be open to conviction and must have a deep and abiding sense of tolerance. It must be hospitable and ready for experiment. . . . It must be grounded in a philosophy whose foundation is on the solidarity of the human race, a philosophy which will not waver when the race happens to be represented by a drunken woman or an idiot boy. Its residents must be emptied of all conceit of opinion and all self-assertion, and ready to arouse and interpret the public opinion of their neighborhood. They must be content to live quietly side by side with their neighbors, until they grow into a sense of relationship and mutual interests.

—Jane Addams, Twenty Years at Hull House,
describing the Settlement House movement

8a. According to Addams, what is the source of the great poverty that can be found in the cities?

_____

_____

_____

_____

8b. Why does Addams argue that the Settlement has to be adaptable?

_____

_____

_____

_____

Document-Based Essay

Part B

DIRECTIONS Using the information in the documents provided and your knowledge of history, write a well-organized essay that includes an introduction, a body of several paragraphs, and a conclusion.

HISTORICAL CONTEXT

Prior to 1880 most immigrants came to the United States from countries with cultures similar to the United States. For the most part, they came from Northern and Western Europe, spoke English, were skilled workers, and were accustomed to a constitutional democracy. Therefore, they assimilated easily into the fabric of American life.

TASK

Using information in the documents and your knowledge of U.S. history, write an essay in which you:

Describe the hardships and obstacles encountered by immigrants arriving after 1880, as well as the opportunities available for their future. In your essay, include a discussion of changing immigration patterns and increased anti-immigrant sentiments that eventually led to restrictive legislation. Also examine the difference between the hopes and dreams of the new immigrants and the realities they faced upon arriving and living in the United States.

GUIDELINES

Be sure to:

• Address all aspects of the *Task* by accurately analyzing and interpreting at least <u>four</u> of the documents.

• Use information provided in the documents in the body of your essay.

• Incorporate relevant outside information in your essay.

• Support your arguments with facts and information that address the theme.

• Be sure to organize your essay in a clear and logical way.

• Establish a framework that is beyond a simple restatement of the *Task* or *Historical Context.*

• Conclude the essay with a summation of the theme.

ACTIVITY (7)   Document-Based Questions

World War I

Document-Based Essay

Part A

DIRECTIONS Analyze the following documents. Use the documents and your knowledge of American history to answer the questions that follow each document. Your answers will help you to write a short essay related to the documents.

Document 1

1a. In terms of this cartoon, what does the phrase "The Boiling Point" suggest? How does it relate to Bismarck's prediction?

_____

_____

_____

_____

_____

_____

_____

_____

2a. What do the men on top of the pot represent, and why are they wearing uniforms?

THE BOILING POINT.

If there is ever another war in Europe, it will come out of some damned silly little thing in the Balkans.
—Prince Otto von Bismarck

_____

_____

_____

_____

_____

_____

Activity 7, World War I, continued

Document 2

> The moment we are about to retreat three faces rise up from the ground in front of us. Under one of the helmets a dark pointed beard and two eyes that are fastened on me. I raise my hand, but I cannot throw into those strange eyes; for one mad moment the whole slaughter whirls like a circus round me . . . then the head rises up . . . and my hand-grenade flies through the air and into him.
>
> We make for the rear, pull wire cradles into the trench and leave bombs behind us with the strings pulled, which ensures us a fiery retreat. The machine-guns are already firing from the next position.
>
> We have become wild beasts. We do not fight, we defend ourselves against annihilation. . . . No longer do we lie helpless, . . . we can destroy and kill to save ourselves . . . to be revenged.
>
> —Erich Maria Remarque, *All Quiet on the Western Front*

From *All Quiet on the Western Front* by Erich Maria Remarque. Copyright 1929, 1930 by Little, Brown and Company; copyright renewed ©1957, 1958 by Erich Maria Remarque. All rights reserved. "Im Westen Nichts Neues" copyright 1928 by Ullstein A.G.; copyright renewed ©1956 by Erich Maria Remarque. Reprinted by permission of the **Estate of Erich Maria Remarque.**

2a. What does Remarque say that the war did to the men who fought in the trenches?

_____

_____

_____

_____

_____

2b. Based on the passage above, what does the soldier in Remarque's novel think about the political problems that prompted the war?

_____

_____

_____

_____

_____

_____

Activity 7, World War I, continued

Document 3

3a. Why does the advertisement on the right warn travellers that if they ride on the *Lusitania* they do so at their own risk?

_____

_____

_____

_____

_____

_____

_____

_____

_____

3b. What happened to the *Lusitania*, and how did that affect popular opinion in the United States?

_____

_____

_____

_____

_____

_____

_____

_____

_____

_____

Steamships

CUNARD

EUROPE ᴠɪᴀ LIVERPOOL

LUSITANIA

Fastest and Largest Steamer
now in Atlantic Service Sails
SATURDAY MAY 1. 10 A M.
Transylvania Fri.,May 7, 5 P.M.
Orduna .. . Tues.,May18,10A.M
Tuscania... Fri.,May 21, 5 P.M
LUSITANIA Sat.,May 29,10 A.M.
Transylvania Fri..June 4, 5 P.M.

Gibraltar Genoa Naples Piraeus
S.S. Carpathia. Thur.. May 13, Noon

NOTICE!

TRAVELLERS intending to embark on the Atlantic voyage are reminded that a state of war exists between Germany and her allies and Great Britain and her allies; that the zone of war includes the waters adjacent to the British Isles; that, in accordance with formal notice given by the Imperial German Government, vessels flying the flag of Great Britain, or of any of her allies, are liable to destruction in those waters, and that travellers sailing in the war zone on ships of Great Britain or her allies do so at their own risk.

Imperial German Embassy
Washington, D C., April 22, 1915

Steck Montage, Inc.

Activity 7, World War I, continued

Document 4

> We intend to begin on the first of February unrestricted submarine warfare. We shall endeavor in spite of this to keep the United States of America neutral. In the event of this not succeeding, we make Mexico a proposal or alliance on the following basis: make war together, make peace together, generous financial support and an understanding on our part that Mexico is to reconquer the lost territory in Texas, New Mexico, and Arizona. The settlement in detail is left to you. You will inform the President (of Mexico) of the above most secretly as soon as the outbreak of war with the United States of America is certain and add the suggestion that he should, on his own initiative, invite Japan to immediate adherence and at the same time mediate between Japan and ourselves. Please call the President's attention to the fact that the ruthless employment of our submarines now offers the prospect of compelling England in a few months to make peace." Signed, ZIMMERMANN.
>
> —telegram from Arthur Zimmermann, German foreign minister to the German ambassador to Mexico (January 16, 1917)

4a. What is the German foreign minister prepared to offer Mexico if Mexico will go to war with the United States? Why might Mexico consider such an offer?

_____

_____

_____

_____

_____

4b. What other country do the Germans plan to attempt to recruit as an ally?

_____

_____

_____

_____

_____

_____

Document 5

The present German submarine warfare against commerce is a warfare against mankind. It is a war against all nations. American ships have been sunk, American lives taken, in ways which it has stirred us very deeply to learn of, but the ships and people of other neutral and friendly nations have been sunk and overwhelmed in the waters in the same way. There has been no discrimination. The challenge is to all mankind. Each nation must decide for itself how it will meet it. The choice we make for ourselves must be made with a moderation of counsel and a temperateness of judgment befitting our character and our motives as a nation. We must put excited feeling away. Our motive will not be revenge or the victorious assertion of the physical might of the nation, but only the vindication of right, of human right, of which we are only a single champion. . . .

The world must be made safe for democracy. Its peace must be planted upon the tested foundations of political liberty. We have no selfish ends to serve. We desire no conquest, no dominion. We seek no indemnities for ourselves, no material compensation for the sacrifices we shall freely make. We are but one of the champions of the rights of mankind. We shall be satisfied when those rights have been made as secure as the faith and the freedom of nations can make them.

—Woodrow Wilson (April 2, 1917)

5a. According to Wilson, what has Germany done that led him to request a declaration of war against it?

_____

_____

_____

_____

_____

5b. What is the purpose of the war from Wilson's perspective?

_____

_____

_____

_____

_____

Activity 7, World War I, continued

Document 6

WORLD WAR I: TROOP STRENGTH

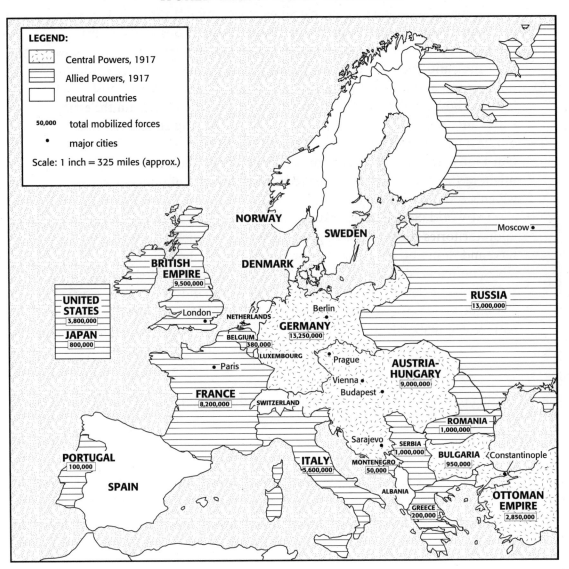

6a. What countries did the United States ally itself with in World War I?

_____

_____

6b. Which European countries remained neutral in the war?

_____

_____

Activity 7, World War I, continued

Document 7

I.   Open covenants [agreements] of peace, openly arrived at, after which there shall be no private international understanding of any kind but diplomacy [negotiations] shall proceed always frankly and in the public view.

II. Absolute freedom of navigation upon the seas, outside territorial waters, alike in peace and in war . . .

III. The removal, so far as possible, of all economic barriers and the establishment of an equality of trade conditions among all nations consenting to the peace . . .

IV. Adequate guarantees given and taken that national armaments [military equipment] will be reduced to the lowest point consistent with domestic safety.

XI. Rumania, Serbia, and Montenegro should be evacuated; occupied territories restored; . . . and international guarantees of the political and economic independence and territorial integrity [completeness] of the several Balkan states should be entered into.

XIII. An independent Polish state should be erected which should include the territories inhabited by indisputable Polish populations, . . . and whose political and economic independence and territorial integrity should be guaranteed . . .

XIV. A general association of nations must be formed under specific covenants for the purpose of affording mutual guarantees of political independence and territorial integrity to great and small nations alike.
    —excerpts from Woodrow Wilson's Fourteen Points (January 18, 1918)

7a. What principle was Wilson asserting by calling for the creation of the countries of Rumania, Serbia, Montenegro, and Poland?

_____

_____

_____

7b. Why did Wilson propose the fourteenth point and what was created in response?

_____

_____

_____

Activity 7, World War I, continued

Document 8

> ARTICLE 231.
> The Allied and Associated Governments affirm and Germany accepts the responsibility of Germany and her allies for causing all the loss and damage to which the Allied and Associated Governments and their nationals have been subjected as a consequence of the war imposed upon them by the aggression of Germany and her allies.
> —excerpt from the Treaty of Versailles (June 28, 1919)

8a. According to the Treaty of Versailles, what country was responsible for World War I? Was that a fair assessment?

_____

_____

_____

_____

_____

_____

_____

_____

8b. Under the terms of the treaty, what is Germany required to pay in reparations?

_____

_____

_____

_____

_____

_____

_____

Activity 7, World War I, continued

Document-Based Essay

Part B

DIRECTIONS Using the information in the documents provided and your knowledge of history, write a well-organized essay that includes an introduction, a body of several paragraphs, and a conclusion.

HISTORICAL CONTEXT
World War I, the "war to end all wars", was very costly in terms of both human lives lost and property destroyed. The Allies lost more than 5 million soldiers, with war costs at more than $145 billion, while the Central Powers lost more than 3.4 million soldiers and the cost was some $63 billion. More than $30 billion in property was destroyed and many economies were ruined.

TASK

Using information in the documents and your knowledge of U.S. history, write an essay in which you:
Discuss the causes of the war in Europe, paying particular attention to the problems in the Balkans. Analyze the reasons the United States entered the World War I despite President Wilson's pledge to remain neutral. Describe the effects of the war upon the soldiers who fought it. Compare Wilson's plan for the post-war world and what actually emerged and the effect this had upon Germany and the long-term prospects for peace.

GUIDELINES

Be sure to:

• Address all aspects of the *Task* by accurately analyzing and interpreting at least <u>four</u> of the documents.

• Use the information provided in the documents in the body of your essay.

• Incorporate relevant outside information throughout the essay.

• Support your arguments with facts and information that address the theme.

• Be sure to organize your essay in a clear and logical way.

• Establish a framework that is beyond a simple restatement of the *Task* or *Historical Context* and conclude the essay with a summation of the theme.

ACTIVITY 8   Document-Based Questions

The Great Depression

Document-Based Essay

Part A

DIRECTIONS Analyze the following documents. Use the documents and your knowledge of American history to answer the questions that follow each document. Your answers will help you to write a short essay related to the documents.

Document 1

> "MARKET CRASHES—PANIC HITS NATION!" one headline blared. . . .
> I couldn't imagine such financial disaster touching my small world; it surely
> concerned only the rich. But by the first week of November I too knew
> differently; along with millions of others across the nation, I was with out
> a job. All that next week I searched for any kind of work that would prevent
> my leaving school. Again it was, "We're firing, not hiring." . . . Finally, on the
> seventh of November I went to school and cleaned out my locker, knowing
> it was impossible to stay on. A piercing chill was in the air as I walked back
> to the rooming house. The hawk had come. I could already feel his wings
> shadowing me.
>
> —Gordon Parks

Quote from "The Hawk Had Come" by Gordon Parks from *Brother Can You Spare a Dime? The Great Depression,
1929–1933* by Milton Metzler. Copyright ©1969 by **Alfred A. Knopf, Inc.** Reprinted by permission of the publisher.

1a. Why would Parks believe that the stock market crash would have no effect on his "small world"?

_____

_____

_____

1b. Why was Parks unable to find a job in the weeks after the stock market crash?

_____

_____

_____

Activity 8, The Great Depression, continued

Document 2

> We in America today, are nearer to the final triumph over poverty that ever before in the history of any land. The poorhouse is vanishing from among us. . . . We shall soon . . . be in sight of the day when poverty will be banished from this nation.
>
> —campaign speech given by Herbert Hoover in 1928
>
> the fundamental business of the country . . . is on a sound and prosperous basis.
>
> —Herbert Hoover during the first week of the stock market crash, 1929
>
> "The Depression is over."
>
> —Herbert Hoover in 1930
>
> "The spread of government destroys initiative [independent action] and thus destroys character. Character is made in the community as well as in the individual by assuming responsibilities, not by escaping them."
>
> —Herbert Hoover in 1930
>
> "We have passed the worst."
>
> —Herbert Hoover in March 1930

2a. Judging by the above quotations, was Hoover realistic in his assessment of the severity of the Great Depression?

_____

_____

_____

_____

_____

2b. What was Hoover's attitude toward government intervention in the economy, based on the quotations above?

_____

_____

_____

_____

_____

Activity 8, The Great Depression, *continued*

Document 3

> I am certain that my fellow Americans expect that on my induction into the Presidency I will address them with a candor and a decision which the present situation of our Nation impels. This is preeminently the time to speak the truth, the whole truth, frankly and boldly. Nor need we shrink from honestly facing conditions in our country today. This great Nation will endure as it has endured, will revive and will prosper. So, first of all, let me assert my firm belief that the only thing we have to fear is fear itself—nameless, unreasoning, unjustified terror which paralyzes needed efforts to convert retreat into advance. In every dark hour of our national life a leadership of frankness and vigor has met with that understanding and support of the people themselves which is essential to victory. I am convinced that you will again give that support to leadership in these critical days. . . .
>
> Our greatest primary task is to put people to work. This is no unsolvable problem if we face it wisely and courageously. It can be accomplished in part by direct recruiting by the Government itself, treating the task as we would treat the emergency of a war, but at the same time, through this employment, accomplishing greatly needed projects to stimulate and reorganize the use of our natural resources.
>
> Hand in hand with this we must frankly recognize the overbalance of population in our industrial centers and, by engaging on a national scale in a redistribution, endeavor to provide a better use of the land for those best fitted for the land. The task can be helped by definite efforts to raise the values of agricultural products and with this the power to purchase the output of our cities. It can be helped by preventing realistically the tragedy of the growing loss through foreclosure of our small homes and our farms.
>
> —Franklin D. Roosevelt, First Inaugural Address (March 4, 1933)

3a. Why does Roosevelt argue that "fear itself" is the greatest problem facing the country?

_____

_____

_____

3b. What is the main thing that the country has to do, according to Roosevelt?

_____

_____

_____

Activity 8, The Great Depression, continued

Document 4

Franklin D. Roosevelt Library

4a. What is Harry Hopkins, head of the Federal Emergency Relief Administration, trying to fix by spending money?

_____

_____

_____

_____

4b. What seems to be Senator Harry Byrd's attitude as demonstrated in the cartoon?

_____

_____

_____

_____

Activity 8, The Great Depression, *continued*

Document 5

> The impact is like a shovelful of fine sand flung against the face. People caught in their own yards grope for the doorstep. Cars come to a standstill, for no light in the world can penetrate that swirling murk. . . . The nightmare is deepest during the storms. But on the occasional bright day and the usual gray day we cannot shake from it. We live with the dust, eat it, sleep with it, watch it strip us of possessions and the hope of possessions. It is becoming the Real. The poetic uplift of spring fades into a phantom of the storied past. The nightmare is becoming life.
>
> —Avis D. Carlson, "Dust"

From "Dust" by Avis D. Carlson from *The New Republic, A Journal of Opinion,* May 1, 1935. Copyright 1935 by **The New Republic.** Reprinted by permission of the publisher.

5a. What is Carlson describing in the above passage?

_____

_____

_____

_____

_____

_____

5b. In response, what did many people do?

_____

_____

_____

_____

_____

_____

_____

_____

Name _____ Class _____ Date _____

Document 6

6a. In the cartoon above, what do the bottles on the table represent?

_____

_____

_____

_____

_____

_____

6b. What do you think the cartoonist thinks about the effectiveness of President Roosevelt's attempts to deal with the Great Depression?

_____

_____

_____

_____

_____

_____

_____

Name _____ Class _____ Date _____

Activity 8, The Great Depression, continued

Document 7

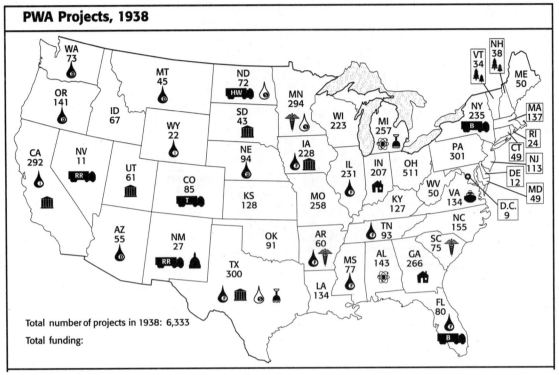

7a. How many PWA projects were underway nationwide in 1938?

_____

_____

_____

_____

_____

7b. In what states did the PWA help build schools?

_____

_____

_____

_____

_____

Activity 8, The Great Depression, continued

Document 8

Select New Deal Programs	
FIRST NEW DEAL, 1933–1934	**PROVISIONS**
Emergency Banking Act	Gave the executive branch the right to regulate banks
Farm Credit Administration (FCA)	Refinanced loans to keep farmers from losing their land
Civilian Conservation Corps (CCC)	Employed young men on public-works projects
Federal Emergency Relief Administration (FERA)	Provided relief to the needy
Agricultural Adjustment Act (AAA) of 1933	Paid farmers to grow fewer crops; later declared unconstitutional
Tennessee Valley Authority (TVA)	Built dams and power plants in the Tennessee Valley region
Home Owners Loan Corporation (HOLC)	Lent money to homeowners to refinance their mortgages
Federal Deposit Insurance Corporation (FDIC)	Insured deposits in individual bank accounts
National Recovery Administration (NRA)	Regulated industry and raised wages and prices
Public Works Administration (PWA)	Set up public-works projects to increase employment
Civil Works Administration (CWA)	Provided federal jobs to the unemployed
Securities and Exchange Commission (SEC)	Regulated the securities market
Federal Housing Administration (FHA)	Insured bank loans for building and repairing homes
SECOND NEW DEAL, 1935–1938	**PROVISIONS**
Works Progress Administration (WPA)	Created jobs in public works, research, and the arts
Rural Electrification Administration (REA)	Provided electricity to rural areas lacking public utilities
National Youth Administration (NYA)	Provided job training and part-time jobs to students
National Labor Relations Act (NLRA)	Recognized labor's right to bargain collectively
Social Security Act	Provided unemployment benefits and retirement pensions
Farm Security Administration (FSA)	Provided loans to help tenant farmers buy land
Agricultural Adjustment Act (AAA) of 1938	Paid farmers to voluntarily limit crop production
Fair Labor Standards Act	Established a minimum wage and a 40-hour workweek

8a. How many New Deal programs were intended to provide work for the unemployed?

_____

_____

_____

_____

8b. What New Deal programs are still in effect today?

_____

_____

_____

_____

Activity 8, The Great Depression, continued

Document-Based Essay

Part B

DIRECTIONS Using the information in the documents provided and your knowledge of history, write a well-organized essay that includes an introduction, a body of several paragraphs, and a conclusion.

HISTORICAL CONTEXT

The 1920s was a decade of economic activity and growth. Many people believed that the prosperity enjoyed by the United States would continue into the future. More people than ever before invested in the stock market, bought items on credit, and took part in the consumerism of the decade. This all came to an end in 1929.

TASK

> Using information in the documents and your knowledge of U.S. history, write an essay in which you:
> Describe the response of the Hoover administration to the onset of the Great Depression. Consider the effects of the depression on people in the United States and what Roosevelt promised to do to help them. Examine the New Deal and whether or not it really helped to bring the country out of the economic crisis. Finally, describe the long-term effect of the Great Depression and the New Deal on the United States.

GUIDELINES

Be sure to:

• Address all aspects of the *Task* by accurately analyzing and interpreting at least <u>four</u> of the documents.

• Use information provided in the documents in the body of your essay.

• Incorporate relevant outside information in your essay.

• Support your arguments with facts and information that address the theme.

• Be sure to organize your essay in a clear and logical way.

• Establish a framework that is beyond a simple restatement of the *Task* or *Historical Context.*

• Conclude the essay with a summation of the theme.

Name _____ Class _____ Date _____

Document-Based Essay

Part A

DIRECTIONS Analyze the following documents. Use the documents and your knowledge of American history to answer the questions that follow each document. Your answers will help you to write a short essay related to the documents.

Document 1

9a. According to the graph, what percentage of Americans believed the United States should have entered World War II in 1939? What reasons might these people have given for U.S. involvement?

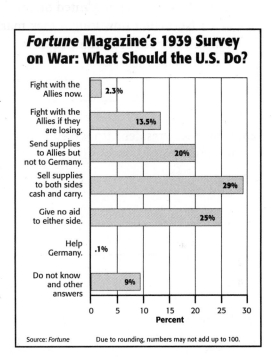

Fortune Magazine's 1939 Survey on War: What Should the U.S. Do?

- Fight with the Allies now. — 2.3%
- Fight with the Allies if they are losing. — 13.5%
- Send supplies to Allies but not to Germany. — 20%
- Sell supplies to both sides cash and carry. — 29%
- Give no aid to either side. — 25%
- Help Germany. — .1%
- Do not know and other answers — 9%

Percent (0, 5, 10, 15, 20, 25, 30)

Source: *Fortune*   Due to rounding, numbers may not add up to 100.

_____

_____

_____

_____

_____

_____

_____

9b. What percentage of Americans believed the United States should support neither side in the struggle? Why would Americans want U.S. neutrality?

_____

_____

_____

_____

_____

_____

_____

_____

Activity 9, World War II, continued

Document 2

Yesterday, December 7, 1941—a date which will live in infamy—the United States of America was suddenly and deliberately attacked by naval and air forces of the Empire of Japan.

The United States was at peace with that nation, and, at the solicitation of Japan, was still in conversation with its government and its Emperor looking toward the maintenance of peace in the Pacific. . . .

As Commander-in-Chief of the Army and Navy I have directed that all measures be taken for our defense, that always will our whole nation remember the character of the onslaught against us.

No matter how long it may take us to overcome this premeditated invasion, the American people, in their righteous might, will win through to absolute victory.

—President Franklin D. Roosevelt (December 8, 1941)

2a. Why does President Roosevelt believe that the date, December 7, 1941, "will live in infamy"? Was he correct?

_____

_____

_____

_____

_____

_____

2b. What makes Roosevelt believe that the Americans will win absolute victory?

_____

_____

_____

_____

_____

_____

_____

Activity 9, World War II, continued

Document 3

We were the second family to go into Tanforan and were assigned to this little room. Our bedroom was a horse stall with doors that were split where the horses would stick their heads out. . . . That was our bedroom. My mother, dad, sister and grandmother lived in the outer edge of this little area. When we were assigned to this area, I sat down with tears in my eyes because, here I am an American citizen being held a prisoner in my own native land.

I forget how many months we spent in Tanforan before we moved on to Topaz. We were the first group to go to Topaz and we traveled by train and everytime we pulled into a railroad station, the blinds had to be drawn; no one wanted to look out anyway because they were scared; there were armed guards and everything. . . . Topaz was located on a dry lake bed of the former Lake Seiver, full of alkaline dust . . . one mile square with every guard tower 100 yards with a sentry up there with his machine gun. Our barracks, since we were the first group, were incomplete; there were no partitions in the toilets and no toilet seats; the food was so-so, but anyway, we set up camp for the other groups that were coming up. . . .

— James Kajiwara, Japanese American Internee

3a. Why was Kajiwara put in an internment camp?

_____

_____

_____

_____

_____

3b. What was life like in the camps?

_____

_____

_____

_____

_____

_____

Activity 9, World War II, continued

Document 4

> The first work I had after the Depression was at a shell-loading plant in Viola, Kentucky. It was between Paducah and Mayfield. They were large shells: anti-aircraft, incendiaries, and tracers. We painted red on the tips of the tracers. My mother, my sister, and myself worked there. Each of us worked a different shift because we had little ones at home. We made a fabulous sum of thirty-two dollars a week. To us it was just an absolute miracle. Before, that, we made nothing.
>
> You won't believe how incredibly ignorant I was, I knew vaguely that a war had started, but had no idea what it meant. . . .
>
> I believe the war was the beginning of my seeing things. You just can't stay uninvolved and not knowing when such a momentous thing is happening. It's just little things that start happening and you put one piece with another. Suddenly, a puzzle begins to take shape.
>
> —Peggy Terry, World War II worker

4a. What did Terry do during World War II?

_____

_____

_____

_____

_____

_____

4b. Was Terry's situation unique? What effect did the war have on women in the United States generally?

_____

_____

_____

_____

_____

_____

_____

Activity 9, World War II, continued

Document 5

> Our landings have failed and I have withdrawn the troops. My decision to attack at this time and place was based upon the best information available. The troops, the air and the Navy did all that bravery and devotion to duty could do. If any blame or fault attaches to the attempt it is mine alone.
> —Supreme Commander Allied Expeditionary Force
> Dwight D. Eisenhower (June 5, 1944)
> *(press release that was never delivered)*

5a. What does this note suggest about the prospects for the Allies prior to the D-Day (June 6, 1944) invasion of Normandy?

_____

_____

_____

_____

_____

_____

_____

_____

_____

5b. According to Eisenhower, who was responsible if the invasion of Normandy failed? Why would he make such a statement?

_____

_____

_____

_____

_____

_____

_____

_____

Activity 9, World War II, continued

Document 6

I had to peer through a haze of sweat, smoke, dust, and mist. I told them [other soldiers] we had to get off the beach and that I'd lead the way. I scurried and scratched along until I got within ten meters of the gun position. Then I unloaded all four of my fragmentation grenades. . . .

After the war, I read about a number of generals and colonels who are said to have wandered about exhorting the troops to advance. . . . I suspect, however that the men were more interested and more impressed by junior officers and NCOs [non-commissioned officers] who were willing to lead them rather than having some general pointing out the direction in which they should go. . . .

When you talk about combat leadership under fire on the beach at Normandy I don't see how the credit can go to anyone other than the company-grade officers and senior NCOs who led the way. It is good to be reminded that there are such men, that there always have been and always will be. We sometimes forget, I think, that you can manufacture weapons, and you can purchase ammunition, but you can't buy valor (courage) and you can't pull heroes off an assembly line.

—Sergeant John Ellery, U.S. Army, 16th Regiment

6a. Based on the above passage, what was the primary factor in the Allied success on D-Day?

_____

_____

_____

_____

_____

6b. What image does Ellery give of Omaha Beach on D-Day?

_____

_____

_____

_____

_____

Activity 9, World War II, continued

Document 7

GERMAN CONCENTRATION AND DEATH CAMPS, 1933–45

From the depths of the mirror, a corpse gazed back at me. The look in his eyes, as they stared into mine, has never left me.

—Elie Wiesel, concentration camp survivor

7a. Why do you think that most of the death camps were located in Poland?

_____

_____

7b. Why does Wiesel describe his reflection as a "corpse" looking back at him?

_____

_____

Activity 9, World War II, continued

Document 8

> The final decision of where and when to use the atomic bomb was up to me.
> Let there be no mistake about it. I regarded the bomb as a military weapon
> and never had any doubt that it should be used. The top military advisors to
> the President recommended its use, and when I talked to Churchill he
> unhesitatingly told me that he favored the use of the atomic bomb if it
> might aid to end the war.
>
> —President Harry S Truman

8a. Is it fair to say that President Truman worried about whether or not to use the atomic
bomb?

_____

_____

_____

_____

_____

_____

_____

_____

8b. According to Truman, what was Churchill's opinion?

_____

_____

_____

_____

_____

_____

_____

_____

_____

Document-Based Essay

Part B

DIRECTIONS Using the information in the documents provided and your knowledge of history, write a well-organized essay that includes an introduction, a body of several paragraphs, and a conclusion.

HISTORICAL CONTEXT

In 1939, Germany invaded Poland marking the beginning of World War II. For most Americans, the fighting in Europe was far away and seemed to have little effect upon life in the United States which, like many countries in the world, was still suffering from the Great Depression. On December 7, 1941, Japan struck the United States naval station at Pearl Harbor, Hawaii, and two days later Germany declared war on the United States.

TASK

Using information in the documents and your knowledge of American history, write an essay in which you:
Describe American attitudes toward the conflict in Europe prior to 1941 and the American entry into the war. Explain why Americans' attitudes and how U.S. entry into the war transformed American society—in both good and bad ways. Also consider the role of the United States in the invasion of Europe. Finally, analyze Truman's decision to use the atomic bomb and its implications for the future.

GUIDELINES

Be sure to:

• Address all aspects of the *Task* by accurately analyzing and interpreting at least <u>four</u> of the documents.

• Use information provided in the documents in the body of your essay.

• Incorporate relevant outside information in your essay.

• Support your arguments with facts and information that address the theme.

• Be sure to organize your essay in a clear and logical way.

• Establish a framework that is beyond a simple restatement of the *Task* or *Historical Context*.

• Conclude the essay with a summation of the theme.

 **ACTIVITY 10**   Document-Based Questions

The Cold War

Document-Based Essay

Part A

DIRECTIONS Analyze the following documents. Use the documents and your knowledge of American history to answer the questions that follow each document. Your answers will help you to write a short essay related to the documents.

Document 1

> The Truman Doctrine
>
> At the present moment in world history nearly every nation must choose between alternative ways of life. . . . One way of life is based upon the will of the majority, and is distinguished by free institutions, representative government, free elections, and . . . freedom from political oppression. The second way of life is based upon the will of the minority forcibly imposed upon the majority. It relies upon terror and oppression . . . and the suppression of personal freedoms. I believe it must be the policy of the United States to support free peoples. . . .
>
> The free peoples of the world look to us for support in maintaining their freedoms. If we falter in our leadership, we may endanger the peace of the world—and we shall surely endanger the welfare of our own nation.
>
> —President Harry S Truman (March 12, 1947)

1a. What distinguishes democracy from communism according to President Truman?

_____

_____

_____

_____

1b. Who does President Truman say the United States should support, and why?

_____

_____

_____

_____

Activity 10, The Cold War, continued

Document 2

The Marshall Plan, 1948–1951

2a. Which countries in Europe did not receive assistance under the Marshall Plan? Why not?

_____

_____

_____

_____

_____

2b. What was the purpose of the Marshall Plan?

_____

_____

_____

_____

_____

_____

Activity 10, The Cold War, continued

Document 3

Editorial Cartoon by Tom Little, 1948; courtesy of the *Nashville Tennessean*

An iron curtain has descended across the Continent. Behind that line lie all the capitals of the ancient states of Central and Eastern Europe. . . . All these famous cities and the populations around them lie in the Soviet sphere and all are subject . . . to a very high and increasing measure of control from Moscow.   —Winston Churchill

3a. In the cartoon, what does the torch lying on the ground represent?

_____

_____

_____

_____

_____

3b. What message is the cartoonist sending, and how does that relate to Winston Churchill's speech?

_____

_____

_____

_____

_____

_____

Activity 10, The Cold War, continued

Document 4

> Article 5 of the North Atlantic Treaty
> April 4, 1949
> The Parties agree that an armed attack against one or more of them in
> Europe or North America shall be considered an attack against them all and
> consequently they agree that, if such an armed attack occurs, each of them,
> in exercise of the right of individual or collective self-defence recognised by
> Article 51 of the Charter of the United Nations, will assist the Party or
> Parties so attacked by taking forthwith, individually and in concert with the
> other Parties, such action as it deems necessary, including the use of armed
> force, to restore and maintain the security of the North Atlantic area.

4a. What did the governments who signed the North Atlantic Treaty which created the
North Atlantic Treaty Organization (NATO) agree to do?

_____

_____

_____

_____

_____

_____

4b. What perceived threat was NATO formed to deal with?

_____

_____

_____

_____

_____

_____

_____

Activity 10, The Cold War, *continued*

Document 5

from Herblock's Special For Today (Simon and Schuster, 1958)

5a. What does "the brink" in the above cartoon refer to? What was "brinkmanship"?

_____

_____

_____

_____

_____

_____

5b. What does the caption suggest about the cartoonist's view of massive retaliation?

_____

_____

_____

_____

_____

_____

_____

Activity 10, The Cold War, continued

Document 6

6a. According to the cartoon above, how many service members died from 1968 to 1972?

_____

_____

_____

_____

_____

_____

6b. Why do you think the United States had difficulty in pulling out of Vietnam?

_____

_____

_____

_____

_____

_____

_____

Activity 10, The Cold War, continued

Document 7

> Behind me stands a wall that encircles the free sectors of this city, part of a vast system of barriers that divides the entire continent of Europe. From the Baltic, south, those barriers cut across Germany in a gash of barbed wire, concrete, dog runs, and guard towers. Farther south, there may be no visible, no obvious wall. But there remain armed guards and checkpoints all the same—still a restriction on the right to travel, still an instrument to impose upon ordinary men and women the will of a totalitarian state. Yet it is here in Berlin where the wall emerges most clearly; here, cutting across your city, where the news photo and the television screen have imprinted this brutal division of a continent upon the mind of the world. Standing before the Brandenburg Gate, every man is a German, separated from his fellow men. Every man is a Berliner, forced to look upon a scar. . . .
>
> General Secretary Gorbachev, if you seek peace, if you seek prosperity for the Soviet Union and Eastern Europe, if you seek liberalization: Come here to this gate! Mr. Gorbachev, open this gate! Mr. Gorbachev, tear down this wall!
>
> —President Ronald Reagan (June 12, 1987)

7a. What made President Reagan believe that General Secretary Gorbachev was interested in seeking peace, prosperity, and liberalization?

_____

_____

_____

_____

_____

7b. According to President Reagan, what does the Berlin Wall represent?

_____

_____

_____

_____

_____

Activity 10, The Cold War, continued

Document 8

NUCLEAR PROLIFERATION IN THE 1980s

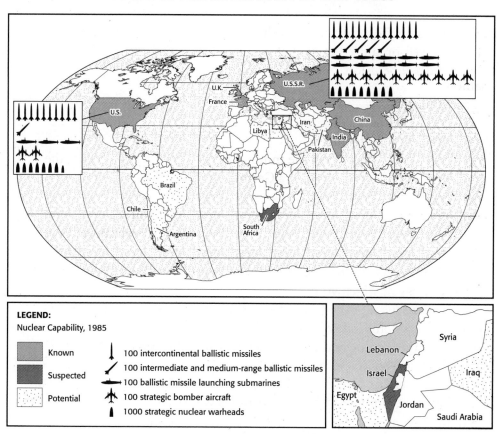

LEGEND:
Nuclear Capability, 1985

▨ Known	↑ 100 intercontinental ballistic missiles
▨ Suspected	⤢ 100 intermediate and medium-range ballistic missiles
▨ Potential	⟷ 100 ballistic missile launching submarines
	✈ 100 strategic bomber aircraft
	▮ 1000 strategic nuclear warheads

8a. Which two countries had the most nuclear weapons in 1985? Why?

_____

_____

_____

_____

8b. How effective was the policy of nuclear deterrence in light of the number of nuclear weapons available?

_____

_____

_____

_____

Activity 10, The Cold War, continued

Document-Based Essay

Part B

DIRECTIONS Using the information in the documents provided and your knowledge of history, write a well-organized essay that includes and introduction, a body, several paragraphs, and a conclusion.

HISTORICAL CONTEXT

The United States and the Soviet Union were allies in World War II against Nazi Germany. However, once Germany was defeated, the reasons for the alliance also ended. What followed was nearly fifty years of conflict that never reached the point of direct armed confrontation between the Soviet Union and the United States.

TASK

Using information in the documents and your knowledge of U.S. history, write an essay in which you:
Analyze the causes of the Cold War, considering the differences in terms of political systems in the United States and the Soviet Union and the perception that each side had of the other. Consider the Soviet actions at the end of World War II and how that affected American foreign policy. Also examine American foreign policy in light of the Cold War. Finally note the increase in the number of nuclear weapons that occurred during the Cold War and the implications this had for American policy-makers.

GUIDELINES

Be sure to:

• Address all aspects of the *Task* by accurately analyzing and interpreting at least <u>four</u> of the documents.

• Use the information provided in the documents in the body of your essay.

• Incorporate relevant outside information throughout the essay.

• Support your arguments with facts and information that address the theme.

• Be sure to organize your essay in a clear and logical way.

• Establish a framework that is beyond a simple restatement of the *Task or Historical Context* and conclude the essay with a summation of the theme.

Name _____ Class _____ Date _____

Document-Based Essay

Part A

DIRECTIONS Analyze the following documents. Use the documents and your knowledge of American history to answer the questions that follow each document. Your answers will help you to write a short essay related to the documents.

Document 1

Plessy v. Ferguson, 163 U.S. 537 (1896)

We consider the underlying fallacy of the plaintiff's argument to consist in the assumption that the enforced separation of the two races stamps the colored race with a badge of inferiority. If this be so, it is not by reason of anything found in the act, but solely because the colored race chooses to put that construction upon it.

—Justice Henry Brown, writing for the majority

(I)n view of the constitution, in the eye of the law, there is in this country no superior, dominant, ruling class of citizens. There is no caste here. Our constitution is color-blind, and neither knows nor tolerates classes among citizens. In respect of civil rights, all citizens are equal before the law. The humblest is the peer of the most powerful. The law regards man as man, and takes no account of his surroundings or of his color when his civil rights as guarantied by the supreme law of the land are involved. . . .

   In my opinion, the judgment this day rendered will, in time, prove to be quite as pernicious (very bad) as the decision made by this tribunal in the *Dred Scott Case.*

—Justice John Marshall Harlan, writing in dissent

1a. Why does the majority opinion maintain that the "Jim Crow law" that forbade Homer Plessy from riding in a "whites only" rail car is constitutional?

_____

_____

1b. According to Harlan, *Plessy* v. *Ferguson* would someday be viewed as a bad decision on the part of the Supreme Court. Was he correct? Explain your answer.

_____

_____

Activity 11, The Civil Rights Movement, continued

Document 2

THE CIVIL RIGHTS MOVEMENT, 1945–1972

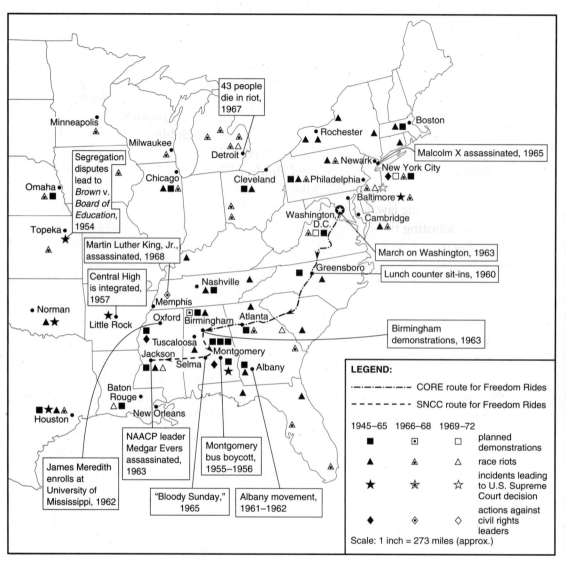

2a. What region of the country had the most activity with regard to civil rights activity?

_____

_____

2b. When was Martin Luther King Jr. assassinated? In what city did it occur?

_____

_____

Name _____ Class _____ Date _____

Document 3

Brown v. *Board of Education*, 347 U.S. 483 (1954)

Today, education is perhaps the most important function of state and local governments. . . . In these days, it is doubtful that any child may reasonably be expected to succeed in life if he is denied the opportunity of an education. Such an opportunity, where the state has undertaken to provide it, is a right which must be made available to all on equal terms.

We come then to the question presented: Does segregation of children in public schools solely on the basis of race, even though the physical facilities and other "tangible" factors may be equal, deprive the children of the minority group of equal educational opportunities? We believe that it does. . . .

Segregation of white and colored children in public schools has a detrimental effect upon the colored children. The impact is greater when it has the sanction of the law, for the policy of separating the races is usually interpreted as denoting the inferiority of the negro group. A sense of inferiority affects the motivation of a child to learn. Segregation with the sanction of law, therefore, has a tendency to [retard] the educational and mental development of negro children and to deprive them of some of the benefits they would receive in a racially integrated school system. . . .

We conclude that, in the field of public education, the doctrine of "separate but equal" has no place. Separate educational facilities are inherently unequal. Therefore, we hold that the plaintiffs and others similarly situated for whom the actions have been brought are, by reason of the segregation complained of, deprived of the equal protection of the laws guaranteed by the Fourteenth Amendment.

—Chief Justice Earl Warren, writing for a unanimous Court

3a. Why does the court's opinion maintain that segregated schools are "inherently unequal"?

_____

_____

_____

3b. According to the court's opinion, what is the most important thing that state and local governments do?

_____

_____

_____

Name _____ Class _____ Date _____

Document 4

> You may well ask: "Why direct action? Why sit-ins, marches, etc.? Isn't nego-
> tiation a better path?" You are exactly right in your call for negotiation.
> Indeed, this is the purpose of direct action. Nonviolent direct action seeks to
> create such a crisis and establish such creative tension that a community that
> has constantly refused to negotiate is forced to confront the issue. It seeks so
> to dramatize the issue that it can no longer be ignored. . . .
>
> We know through painful experience that freedom is never voluntarily
> given by the oppressor; it must be demanded by the oppressed. Frankly, I
> have never yet engaged in a direct action movement that was "well timed,"
> according to the timetable of those who have not suffered unduly from the
> disease of segregation. For years now I have heard the words [sic]"Wait!" It
> rings in the ear of every Negro with a piercing familiarity. This "Wait" has
> almost always meant "Never." We must come to see with the distinguished
> jurist of yesterday that "justice too long delayed is justice denied."
>
> —Reverend Martin Luther King Jr.,
> *Letter from a Birmingham Jail* (April 16, 1963)

4a. What does King hope to accomplish by "direct action"?

_____

_____

_____

_____

_____

_____

4b. According to King, what would happen if he gave up direct action?

_____

_____

_____

_____

_____

_____

Activity 11, The Civil Rights Movement, continued

Document 5

This afternoon, following a series of threats and defiant statements, the presence of Alabama National Guardsmen was required on the University of Alabama to carry out the final and unequivocal order of the United States District Court of the Northern District of Alabama. That order called for the admission of two clearly qualified young Alabama residents who happened to have been born Negro. . . .

We are confronted primarily with a moral issue. It is as old as the scriptures and is as clear as the American Constitution.

The heart of the question is whether all Americans are to be afforded equal rights and equal opportunities, whether we are going to treat our fellow Americans as we want to be treated. If an American, because his skin is dark, cannot eat lunch in a restaurant open to the public, if he cannot send his children to the best public school available, if he cannot vote for the public officials who will represent him, if, in short, he cannot enjoy the full and free life which all of us want, then who among us would be content to have the color of his skin changed and stand in his place? Who among us would then be content with the counsels of patience and delay?

One hundred years of delay have passed since President Lincoln freed the slaves, yet their heirs, their grandsons, are not fully free. They are not yet freed from the bonds of injustice. They are not yet freed from social and economic oppression. And this Nation, for all its hopes and all its boasts, will not be fully free until all its citizens are free. . . .

Next week I shall ask the Congress of the United States to act, to make a commitment it has not fully made in this century to the proposition that race has no place in American life or law.

—President John F. Kennedy (June 11, 1963)

5a. Did President Kennedy believe that the United States had achieved its full potential with regard to civil rights for all of its citizens?

_____

_____

_____

5b. What prompted Kennedy to make his address to the nation?

_____

_____

_____

Activity 11, The Civil Rights Movement, continued

Document 6

PRC Archive

Collection of Janice L. and David J. Frent/PRC Archive

6a. What is the difference between the two buttons in the pictures above? Do they represent different approaches to the struggle for equal rights? Explain your answer.

_____

_____

_____

_____

_____

_____

6b. Who gave a famous address at the March on Washington? What was it called?

_____

_____

_____

_____

_____

_____

Activity 11, The Civil Rights Movement, continued

Document 7

I speak tonight for the dignity of man and the destiny of Democracy. I urge
every member of both parties, Americans of all religions and of all colors,
from every section of this country, to join me in that cause.

At times, history and fate meet at a single time in a single place to shape
a turning point in man's unending search for freedom. So it was at
Lexington and Concord. So it was a century ago at Appomattox. So it was
last week in Selma, Alabama. There, long suffering men and women peace-
fully protested the denial of their rights as Americans. Many of them were
brutally assaulted. One good man—a man of God—was killed. . . .

Many of the issues of civil rights are very complex and most difficult.
But about this there can and should be no argument: every American citizen
must have an equal right to vote. There is no reason which can excuse the
denial of that right. There is no duty which weighs more heavily on us than
the duty we have to insure that right. Yet the harsh fact is that in many
places in this country men and women are kept from voting simply because
they are Negroes. . . .

We have all sworn an oath before God to support and to defend that
Constitution. We must now act in obedience to that oath. Wednesday, I will
send to Congress a law designed to eliminate illegal barriers to the right to
vote. . . .

But even if we pass this bill the battle will not be over. What happened
in Selma is part of a far larger movement which reaches into every section
and state of America. It is the effort of American Negroes to secure for
themselves the full blessings of American life. Their cause must be our cause
too. Because it's not just Negroes, but really it's all of us, who must overcome the crippling legacy of bigotry and injustice.

And we shall overcome.
—President Lyndon B. Johnson, announcing his proposal
for a voting rights act (March 15, 1965)

7a. What was the significance of President Johnson's use of the phrase "we shall overcome" in his address?

_____

_____

7b. According to Johnson, why must government officials support the right of African
Americans to vote?

_____

_____

Activity 11, The Civil Rights Movement, continued

Document 8

> I *am* for violence if non-violence means we continue postponing a solution
> to the American black man's problems—just to *avoid* violence. I don't go for
> non-violence if it also means a delayed solution. To me a delayed solution is
> a non-solution. Or I'll say it another way. If it must take violence to get the
> black man his human rights in this country, I'm *for* . . .violence. I tell sincere
> white people, 'Work in conjunction with us—each of us working among our
> own kind.' Let sincere white individuals find all other white people they can
> who feel as they do—and let them form their own all-white groups, to work
> trying to convert other white people who are thinking and acting so racist.
> Let sincere whites go and teach non-violence to white people.
>
> —Malcolm X, *The Autobiography of Malcolm X*

8a. When is violence justified, according to Malcolm X?

_____

_____

_____

_____

_____

_____

_____

8b. What role did Malcolm X believe white Americans should fulfill?

_____

_____

_____

_____

_____

_____

_____

_____

Document-Based Essay

Part B

DIRECTIONS Using the information in the documents provided and your knowledge of history, write a well-organized essay that includes an introduction, a body of several paragraphs, and a conclusion.

HISTORICAL CONTEXT

In the aftermath of the Civil War, many states passed laws to legally separate African Americans and white Americans in education, public accommodations, restaurants— even cemeteries were segregated in some areas. The Supreme Court ruled such laws were valid. Throughout the 1900s many people struggled to achieve full equality.

TASK

Using information in the documents and your knowledge of U.S. history, write an essay in which you:
Explore the change in the position taken by the Supreme Court with regard to civil rights and the implications this had on the Civil Rights Movement. Consider the different approaches to the problem of civil rights for African Americans promoted by Martin Luther King Jr. and Malcolm X. Finally, describe the political response that led to legislative action on behalf of equal rights.

GUIDELINES

Be sure to:

• Address all aspects of the *Task* by accurately analyzing and interpreting at least <u>four</u> of the documents.

• Use information provided in the documents in the body of your essay.

• Incorporate relevant outside information throughout the essay.

• Support your arguments with facts and information that address the theme.

• Be sure to organize your essay in a clear and logical way.

• Establish a framework that is beyond a simple restatement of the *Task* or *Historical Context* and conclude the essay with a summation of the theme.